SALZBURG

Town Guide

Text
WILFRIED SCHABER

English translation
Gail Schamberger

Residenz Verlag

CONTENTS

The Fortress and the Old Town, in the centre Cathedral and Squares

Chronological Table of the Town's History

Prehistoric and Roman times: Isolated finds from the Stone Age. Salt-mining on the Dürrnberg, by Hallein, and the resultant trade led to a concentrated population in the Hallstatt period (c. 1000 — 450 B.C.). Flourishing Celtic culture in the la Tène period (450 — beginning of the Christian era), a prosperous settlement on the Dürrnberg; the rich funeral furniture is exhibited in the Celtic Museum in Hallein (16 km. south of Salzburg). The kingdom of Noricum was subjugated in 15 B.C. by Tiberius, and under the Emperor Claudius (41—54 A.D.) it became a Roman province, receiving its municipal constitution as Juvavum (Salzburg).

c. 470: St. Severin visits a monastery in Salzburg; after the departure of large sections of the Roman population, only the Nonnberg terrace is inhabited. The existence of a community of monks until the arrival of Rupert is possible.

696: St. Rupert comes to Salzburg, founds the convent, revives the monastery of St. Peter and builds a church of St. Peter.

8th century: Salzburg is for a time the seat of the Dukes of Bavaria, becomes a bishopric, then an archbishopric, extremely rich in landed property. The most important bishops are St. Virgil, an Irishman, and Arno. Art flourishes, as the Cathedral of St. Virgil, a notable scriptorium and objects of the goldsmith's art (the Tassilo chalice) demonstrate.

c. 1060: During the investiture struggle between the Emperor and the Pope, the Fortress is completed.

1167: The Emperor Frederick Barbarossa imposes the imperial ban on Salzburg. The town is burnt down. 12th century: flourishing period for art, important scriptorium, frescoes; construction of a magnificent new cathedral, rebuilding of the town.

13th — 15th centuries: First city wall (13th c.), extension of the archiepiscopal principality. Art flourishes around 1400 ("Schöne Madonnen") and around 1500, promoted by the now prosperous middle classes. Michael Pacher erects two great altars.

16th century: Cardinal Matthäus Lang is the first Renaissance prince on the bishop's throne of Salzburg (1519–1540). Johann von Staupitz, Martin Luther's former superior and friend, is Abbot of St. Peter's (1522—1524). Peasants' Wars, Reformation. The composer Paul Hofhaymer (†1524) and the physician and chemist Paracelsus (†1541) are active in Salzburg.

17th century: Archbishop Wolf Dietrich (1587–1612) changes the face of the town; his successors work until the end of the century on the realisation of the new building plans. He has transformed mediaeval Salzburg into the "Rome of the North". Italian artists are entrusted with the principal building projects.

18th century: Archbishop Johann Ernst Thun (1687—1709) dismisses the leading Italian artists and delegates the planning of all the building to be done in the town to Johann Bernhard Fischer von Erlach. Johann Lukas von Hildebrandt takes over from Fischer. The leading painters are Johann Michael Rottmayr and Martin Johann Schmidt. Older churches are decorated and furnished in late baroque or rococo style. In 1731/32, under Archbishop Firmian, more than 20,000 Protestants are forced to emigrate. On 27th January 1756, Wolfgang Amadeus Mozart is born at no. 9, Getreidegasse.

1803: Secularisation; the ecclesiastical principality of Salzburg ceases to exist. Grand Duke Ferdinand III of Tuscany becomes the first Elector of Salzburg. When he returns via Würzburg to Florence in 1805, he takes with him the extremely valuable treasures of the archbishopric. 1806—1809: Salzburg is for the first time in Austrian hands; choice items of what treasure is left are taken to Vienna. During the Bavarian occupation (1810—1815), the last remaining objects of value end up in Munich. These years brought immense losses for the art collection of the archbishopric.

1816: Salzburg belongs definitively to Austria.

1818: A great fire destroys the New Town. Town and countryside are discovered by Romantic artists. On 25th December, in the Church of St. Nicholas in Oberndorf by Salzburg, the carol "Silent Night" is sung for the first time.

1850: Salzburg becomes an independent crownland (of the Austrian empire) and is given its own government.

1860: Prohibition of any building within the area of the town fortifications rescinded. This gave rise to the demolishing of ramparts and gates and to the expansion of the town in the Mirabell district and the area around the station. Railway line Vienna—Salzburg—Munich opened.

1862—1866: The fortifications in the Mirabell quarter of the town are demolished, and the Salzach is regulated.

1894: The Linzer Gate is pulled down.

1917: Establishing of the Festival Association.

1920: First "Everyman" performance in the Cathedral Square.

1926: Building started on Small Festival Hall (Clemens Holzmeister)

1944/45: Bombardment of the town; the Cathedral, Kai and Gstätten quarters of the Old Town are badly hit, and the New Town sustains extensive damage.

1953: The "Arbeitsgruppe 4" (Holzbauer, Kurrent, Spalt) erects the parish church in Parsch, and, in 1961, the College of the Precious Blood in Aigen, both buildings establishing modern architectural trends in Salzburg.

1956—1960: Building of the Large Festival Hall, designed by Clemens Holzmeister.

1962: Re-establishment of Salzburg University.

1967: Order for the preservation of the Old Town of Salzburg, providing the basis for the conservation of the uniquely beautiful appearance of the town.

1971—1976: Building of St. Virgil cultural centre, designed by Wilhelm Holzbauer.

1982: Building started on the Faculty of Natural Sciences in Freisaal (Wilhelm Holzbauer).

THE OLD TOWN

The Cathedral Precincts ①

The Cathedral precincts form the dominating centre of Salzburg. The broad, generous arrangement of the squares and the immense edifices with their splendid façades stand in strong contrast to the piecemeal-built "Bürgerviertel" (burghers' quarter) with its narrow streets full of corners. The conditions of this expansive layout, uninterrupted by diminutive structures, already existed in embryo in the Middle Ages. In the place of today's early baroque Cathedral stood the Romanesque episcopal church; to the north of it, on the Residenzplatz, stretched the cathedral cemetery. The square to the west of the cathedral was also free of buildings, and the area to the south of it was occupied by the monastery. Archbishop Wolf Dietrich von Raitenau (1587—1612), a greatnephew of the Medici Pope Pius IV and educated in Italy, conceived, with the help of Vincenzo Scamozzi (1552—1616) from Vicenza, a pupil of Palladio, that magnificent building project with its Italian-style spaciousness, to which this "Italian" town north of the Alps — also called the "Rome of the North" — owed its uniqueness. With his unprecedented passion for building — though more destructive than constructive — Wolf Dietrich eradicated the traces of mediaeval buildings from the face of Salzburg. He had the huge Romanesque minster pulled down and, to the horror of his contemporaries, caused the revered graves of the bishops to be demolished. The cathedral cemetery, in which the citizens of Salzburg had for centuries buried their dead, was levelled, and the monastery fell under the pickaxe. Wolf Dietrich was able to realise his grand projects only in part, and it was Marcus Sitticus and Paris Lodron, his successors on the bishop's throne, who gave shape to his visions.

THE CATHEDRAL

The dark massive walls of the early baroque Cathedral call to mind a stronghold — a divine stronghold. Leaving aside the dome and the façade, one is reminded of the Middle Ages, of great solid walls with unadorned windows cut in them and of gloomy vaults. The predominant building material is stone, the local "Nagelfluh"; in these ashlar walls, art has re-created the Mönchsberg rock with its "cave chapels" and ennobled it with a marble façade. Although this cathedral (begun in 1614) designed by the North Italian Santino Solari (1576—1646) was considered modern, it too, like everything else in Salzburg, bears strong marks of the local traditions. On the one hand, Solari's walls conform to the sombre aspect of the mediaeval minster; on the other, the old "cave chapels" of the Mönchsberg rock offer an ever-varied theme.

The marble façade, which is perhaps based on sketches by Scamozzi, is merely affixed like an ornament to the main body of the building, and looks like the costly setting of a venerated relic. The façade and the main body are not conceived as an organic unit in the architectonic sense (there is no angle from which both may be viewed at once); their relationship is that of an allegedly ancient vessel to which particular historical significance is imputed only due to the richly-worked gold mounting.

The Interior: The nave is a broad, barrel-vaulted, dimly-lit hall ending in a bright triple apse under the dome. While the nave receives only indirect daylight, the walls of the "clover-leaf" choir are pierced by 43 windows which flood it with light. Four side-chapels with oratories above them line the nave on either side; with their Roman arches, double-doored balconies and pilasters, they present an austere, almost secular façade — the nave looks like a stately avenue which is there simply to accompany and escort the visitor to the central crossing.

Decoration and furnishings: When the Cathedral was consecrated in 1628, the marble twin-towered façade was not yet completed, and the octagonal turrets on top of the towers were built only in 1652—1655. In 1660, Bartholomäus Opstal sculpted statues of the patron saints of the province, SS. Rupert and Virgil, these being the outer two at the entrance arcades; the inner two, SS. Peter

The Cathedral

and Paul, more animated in appearance, are the work of Bernhard Mandl, 1697/98. In the middle storey of the façade, decorated with Ionic pilasters, are the figures of the Four Evangelists. The pediment with the coats of arms of the two archbishops responsible for the building, Marcus Sitticus (1612—1619) and Paris Lodron (1619—1653), is crowned by a figure of Christ flanked by Moses and Elijah. These sculptures are attributed to the "Master of the Residenz fountain", Tommaso Garuo Allio. The bronze doors of the three portals, portraying Faith, Hope and Love, were executed in 1957/58 by Toni Schneider-Manzell (left-hand door), Giacomo Manzù (centre door) and Ewald Mataré (right-hand door).

The Gothic font to the left of the entrance is a relic of the mediaeval minster and was cast in bronze by Meister Heinrich in 1321; it rests on four 12th century bronze lions. The pulpit (1958) is by Toni Schneider-Manzell. The high altar and those in the apses are early 17th century marble-work, the sculptures are by Konrad Asper and Hans Pernegger the Younger. The painting of the Resurrection on the high altar is the work of Donato Mascagni; the altar painting in the south apse showing "The Snow-Miracle of the Virgin" was done by Ignazio Solari, the architect's son; the "Vision of St. Francis" on the north altar is also by Mascagni. The altars in the side-chapels are the work of Giovanni Antonio Dario, and were erected in 1670. The altar paintings in the first three south chapels (from W to E) — "St. Roch and St. Sebastian", "St. Karl Borromäus" and "St. Martin und St. Jerome" — are by J. Heinrich Schönfeld (1609—1683). Karel Škreta (1610—1674) painted the "Pentecost" in the last side-chapel. The altar paintings in the north chapels (from W to E) are "The Baptism of Christ" by Frans de Neve (1672—1674 in Salzburg), "St. Anne with the Virgin Mary and the Christchild" by Jonathan Sandrart (1606—1688), "The Transfiguration of Christ", a copy by Johann Fackler (18th c.), and in the last chapel "The Crucifixion of Christ" by Karel Škreta.

Donato Mascagni, with the help of his pupil Ignazio Solari, painted the cartouches and medaillons, with their wide stucco frames, in the nave and choir. In dome and choir, the paintings were completed for the consecration in 1628. The Stations of the Cross and the ceiling paintings in the chapels were the work of Ludwig Glötzle in the years 1881—1895. In 1955, exact copies were made of the frescoes in the dome, which had been demolished by a bomb during the Second World War. The series of paintings is ordered Christologically: in the dim vaults of the nave are the Life and Sufferings of Christ; the Laying in the Tomb and the Descent into Purgatory are in the presbytery, the Resurrection of Christ is the theme for the high altar. The dome shows scenes from the Old Testament. The south apse is reserved for the life of the Virgin Mary, the north apse bears scenes from the life of St. Francis.

The Crypt: The rebuilding of the dome after war damage offered an opportunity for a comprehensive restoration and for an archaeological exploration of

Cathedral interior, looking towards the high altar

the Cathedral. After the excavations were completed, a crypt and a burial vault
for the bishops of Salzburg were constructed underneath the crossing (staircase
in the south apse), incorporating excavated remains of previous walls.

The mediaeval cathedral: After his arrival in Salzburg in 696, St. Rupert (†716
or 718) erected a Church of St. Peter and revived the existing monastery. It is
not yet certain where this church stood — in the St. Peter's Monastery precincts
(cf. early history of that chapter) or in the Cathedral precincts; no building complex has yet been discovered that could with certainty be ascribed to the period
of St. Rupert (c. 700). In 739, in the process of St. Boniface's re-organisation of
the Bavarian church, Salzburg became a bishopric. The first recognisable cathedral building is that of the scholarly Irish Abbot (and later Bishop) of Salzburg,
Virgil (abbot 746/47, bishop from 749, †784). The building of this church "of
an astonishing size", as sources report, was begun after 760, and must have been
completed in 774, when the remains of St. Rupert were brought ceremoniously
from Worms, where he died, to Salzburg. Virgil's cathedral, 66 m. long, was one
of the largest churches in the Frankish kingdom. Excavations provided a basis
for the reconstruction of its ground plan; a remarkable feature is the "clover-
leaf" interior of the apse. This building remained substantially unchanged until
the time of Bishop Hartwig (c. 1000). Bishop Arno (784—821, first archbishop
in 798) had incorporated a west crypt; in 850, following a fire, the Liupramm
Chapel was built on to the south side, overlaying Virgil's grave, which was in
the south wall, and which was then forgotten, not to be rediscovered until 1181.
Under Bishop Hartwig (991—1023), extensive alterations were made. The nave
was extended to the west by about 33 m., and to the east a deep choir with crypt
was added. Bishop Konrad I (1106—1147) had extremely high west towers erected
in 1127. All these alterations and renovations still took into account the basic
proportions of Virgil's cathedral. But when Bishop Konrad III (1177—1183)
began rebuilding *a fundamento*, only the west towers remained of the previous
building. This Romanesque cathedral, which must have been consecrated in
about 1200, remained standing until 1598, when Wolf Dietrich had it pulled
down following insignificant fire damage. 110 m. long, it had surpassed all its
predecessors; its eastern end, including the transept, the dome over the crossing
and the transept towers, was modelled on the Rhenish imperial cathedrals. It had
a triple nave, and a row of chapels on the north side and the monastery cloister
adjoining the south nave make even five naves seem a possibility. After the old
minster had been demolished, Archbishop Wolf Dietrich had a monumental
new cathedral planned by Scamozzi, but this project was not realised. In 1610,
the foundations were laid for a cathedral standing north-south, but its erection
was prevented by the overthrow of Wolf Dietrich in 1612. His successors, Marcus Sitticus and Paris Lodron, then realised (1614—1628) the more modest
design by Santino Solari.

THE ARCHAEOLOGICAL MUSEUM

From the north arcades, a staircase leads down to the archaeological museum, to the excavation area in front of the baroque façade; it is open to visitors from Easter until October. Finds are exhibited in glass cases, and there are commentaries explaining the remains of walls which were part of the previous cathedral buildings.

THE CATHEDRAL MUSEUM WITH THE WUNDERKAMMER
(closet of rarities)

The entrance is on the right of the vestibule. The museum is installed in the south oratories, and the archiepiscopal closet of rarities takes up the rooms above the south arches; further show-rooms are in the second storey of the building adjoining the Cathedral Square. In the years following 1803, when the ecclesiastic principality ceased to exist, the Cathedral treasure was distributed in

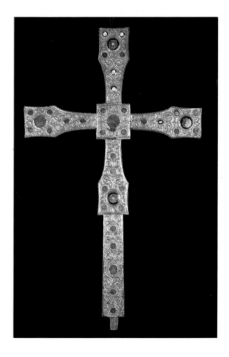

"Rupertuskreuz"
in the Cathedral museum,
England, 8th c.

all directions, and a substantial part of it is preserved today in the Silver Chamber of the Palazzo Pitti in Florence. The items remaining in Salzburg are exhibited in the Cathedral museum, and have been supplemented by valuable examples of local works of art from the diocesan estate. The so-called "Rupertuskreuz" (Rupert crucifix) is a monumental work of mediaeval art; it is of Northumbrian manufacture, 8th century, and was possibly brought to Salzburg by Bishop Virgil. Another significant work is a 12th century Byzantine staurotheca on a Gothic mount, said to have been the cross on which the Hungarian monarchs swore their coronation oath. There are many beautifully crafted mediaeval reliquaries, and Wolf Dietrich's monstrance (1596) and his missal-cover, by the court goldsmith Hans Karl, deserve special mention. Altar-cloths, vestments and utensils from the baroque era complete the mediaeval collection, the diamond monstrance of 1697 being a particularly precious item. The closet of rarities was installed by Archbishop Guidobald Thun. Its present form, with the original show-cases, is a successful reconstruction. These "closets of rarities" were the predecessors of our museums — the entire world of art and nature was mirrored in them. Every precious material was represented: ore, precious stones, exotic nuts, corals and ivory, both in their natural state and transformed by the much-admired skill of craftsmen.

THE CATHEDRAL SQUARE (Domplatz)

The Cathedral façade was completed under Archbishop Guidobald Thun, who also had the Cathedral arcades built in 1660 by Giovanni Antonio Dario. These connect the Cathedral, like marble bridges, with the Residenz and the "Gallery". The arches are crowned with heads of wild horses, an allusion to Guidobald's heraldic beast, the unicorn. The arcades, which take up motifs from the Cathedral façade in considerably reduced proportion, accomplished the definitive separation of the main body from the west façade, making it a kind of "display wall". An intimate inner courtyard was thus formed, with no wide open access roads, and narrow arcades blocking the approaches. This is where the annual performance of Hugo von Hofmannsthal's "Everyman" takes place — the play of the life and death of the rich man. In the centre of the square stands the statue of the Virgin Mary, by Wolfgang and Johann Baptist Hagenauer, constructed in 1766—1771 at the behest of Archbishop Sigismund Schrattenbach. The figures round the pedestal embody Wisdom, the Church, Angel and Devil, each, according to its nature, perceiving the mystery of the Immaculate Conception.

THE KAPITELPLATZ

This square lies to the south of the Cathedral on the site of the old monastery. On the right, to the west, it is bounded by wings of St. Peter's Monastery, and leading off it to the east is the narrow Kapitelgasse with the chapter-houses

LEOPOLDVS PRINCEPS ME EXSTRVXIT

The ornamental horse-pond on the Kapitelplatz

erected by Wolf Dietrich for the canons. One is strongly aware of the town's natural surroundings from this square, which is dominated by the Festungsberg and the menacing Fortress. Mountain and fountain are linked by the outline of an ornamental wall, out of which water flows over steps to fill the ornamental horse-pond with its surrounding balustrades; in the niche, mounted on a horse, appears Neptune, the central figure of the display. The chronogram "LeopoLDVs prInCeps Me eXstrVXIt" (Prince Leopold built me) reveals the date of construction, 1732; the creator was the supervisor of the archiepiscopal gardens, Franz Anton Danreiter; Neptune is a splendid work by the Salzburg sculptor Joseph Anton Pfaffinger.

THE RESIDENZPLATZ

While the Domplatz lends itself to more intimate festive occasions, and the Kapitelplatz takes its character from the natural elements of water and mountain, the Residenzplatz was the setting for official proceedings and events of the principality. It borders on the Burghers' Town, and is marked by the commanding presence of the gloomy Cathedral and the austere palaces of the administration of the principality. This atmosphere of restraint is relieved by the Residenz fountain; snorting steeds spring forth from the fissures of the spouting rock, three primitive sturdy giants, still rooted in the stone, hold up the lower basin, in which fish balance on their tails the upper basin with the Triton, from whose conch-shell trumpet the jet of water springs triumphantly. Archbishop Guidobald Thun had the fountain erected in 1656—1661; the sculptor may have been Tommaso Garuo Allio from the Intelvi Valley near Lake Como.

THE NEW RESIDENZ WITH THE GLOCKENSPIEL (carillon)

This forms the eastern side of the square. Wolf Dietrich had this palace built, starting in 1588, for himself and his guests. Later, Archbishop Max Gandolf Kuenburg added south and west wings, and in 1702 Johann Ernst Thun heightened the tower and installed the carillon. State rooms on the second floor (formerly Wolf Dietrich's living quarters) are on exhibition; they boast particularly fine coloured stucco-work by Elia Castello (1600—1603). The "Saal der Tugenden", the antechamber, shows in stucco the Christian virtues of Faith, Hope and Love, with, in the spandrels, the Cardinal Virtues of fortitude, justice, prudence and temperance. The ceiling of the next room, the "Gloriensaal", is ornamented with angelic choirs and scenes from the New Testament. The "Ständesaal" (so called since 1620) contains scenes from Roman history: the "Sacrifice of Marcus Curtius", "Horatius Cocles defending the bridge over the Tiber", and "Mucius Scaevola putting his hand in the fire". The "Feldherrensaal" was possibly Wolf Dietrich's bedchamber; the spandrels are decorated with relief busts of Charlemagne, Juan d'Austria, Karl V and Gottfried von Bouillon. Adjoining is a bathroom with a tiled cupola.

The Residenzplatz with the fountain, the New Residenz and the Glockenspiel tower, on the left St. Michael's Church, in the background the Mozartplatz

The observation gallery round the carillon is accessible on a guided tour (times displayed at the north entrance on the Mozartplatz). Archbishop Johann Ernst Thun acquired the carillon (originally intended for the town of Breda) in Amsterdam in 1696, and in 1702 local artisans furnished it with a mechanism which is still responsible for certain dissonances. It plays three times a day — at 7 a.m., 11 a.m. and 6 p.m. The titles of the tunes can be read at the north-east corner of the Residenz.

THE RESIDENZ　　　　　　　　　　　　　　　　　　　　②

The archiepiscopal residence is a massive complex of buildings occupying the entire area between the Residenzplatz and the Sigmund-Haffner-Gasse, the Franciscan church and the Alter Markt (old market-place). The restrained arrangement of its façades, which on the Residenzplatz side have an almost fortified look, is typical of the modest outward aspect of Salzburg architecture. The reception rooms of the archiepiscopal court are set in the quadrangle surrounding the courtyard of arcades. The newer Toscana Wing in the Sigmund-Haffner-Gasse is to house university institutes at the end of the 1980's.

Decoration and furnishings: The main portal, on the Residenzplatz, displays the coats of arms of the various archbishops responsible for building. The inner courtyard, which resembles a high shaft, is given its character by the colossal pilasters and the portico in the west wall, in which opens a shady grotto-like niche where Hercules is shown overpowering the Hydra of Lerna. Two ibexes — the heraldic beasts of Marcus Sitticus — spout water, with a singular air of indifference to proceedings. The fountain was erected in 1615, the figure of Hercules being a rather earlier work (c. 1606) from Wolf Dietrich's garden, "Dietrichsruh". In the left side of the portico is the entrance up to the *piano nobile*.

The State Rooms: There is a guided tour of these. The Carabinierisaal, which looks on to the Cathedral Square, dates from the time of Wolf Dietrich; it was the room used by the bodyguard, and served also as theatre and banqueting hall. The ceiling frescoes are major works by Johann Michael Rottmayr (1689/90), the stucco is by Francesco and Carlo Antonio Brenno. The centrepiece portrays Neptune commanding the winds in order to protect Aeneas on his voyage to Italy; the side frescoes depict the Calydonian hunt and Vulcan's forge. In 1709, Archbishop Franz Anton Harrach commissioned Johann Michael Rottmayr and Martino Altomonte to do the paintings in the reception rooms, supervised by the architect Johann Lukas von Hildebrandt. The scheme of the pictures, which portray events from the life of Alexander the Great, is an allusion to the lordly virtues of the Prince-Archbishop Franz Anton Harrach.

The central painting in the Rittersaal is by Johann Michael Rottmayr (1714), and shows Alexander taming his warhorse Bucephalus "without blows or spurs", alluding to a personal motto of Prince Harrach. The ceiling paintings in the conference room are the work of Martino Altomonte (1710). The centre picture shows Alexander in the Battle of Granicus. The paintings in the antechamber are also by Altomonte, the main, circular picture showing the cutting of the Gordian knot. Rottmayr completed in 1711 the ceiling paintings in the audience chamber, "Alexander receiving the allegiance of the town of Byblos" being the main theme. The walls are hung with Brussels tapestries with the coat of arms of Wolf Dietrich and themes taken from heroic Roman history. Worthy of note is an astronomical upright clock by the court clockmaker of Salzburg, Bentele (c.1730). The study and the private treasury were decorated by Altomonte, with "Alexander sacrificing in the temple of Jerusalem" in the centre of the ceiling. The ceiling painting in the bedchamber is by Rottmayr, and portrays "the vigilance of Alexander", who never gave himself up to deep, unconscious sleep; just as the vigilant crane holds a stone in its raised claw, so Alexander's fingers clasp a silver ball which, if it fell into the metal basin below, would immediately indicate a lapse of vigilance.

The frescoes in the chapel and the "Schöne Galerie" are also by Rottmayr. The ceiling fresco, dated 1711, is an allegory of the arts and sciences. Johann Lukas von Hildebrandt designed the richly-framed niche above the fireplace for the "Jüngling vom Magdalensberg". The original Roman bronze from the early 1st century A.D. was discovered in 1502 on the Magdalensberg in Carinthia, and acquired by the Salzburg Archbishop Matthäus Lang von Wellenburg. After the secularisation of the archbishopric, a copie from the 16th century was taken to Vienna, another copy remained in Salzburg. The Roman original is lost. The "Schöne Galerie" housed parts of the archiepiscopal collection of paintings. Rottmayr had already furnished the drawing-room with ceiling paintings in 1689; here is depicted the banquet of the gods at the wedding of Thetis. The "Weisser

The conference room, one of the state rooms in the Residenz

Saal" was stuccoed in 1776 by Peter Pflauder, in accordance with classicist taste. In the Kaisersaal hang portraits, dating from about 1720, of emperors from the House of Habsburg; from this room, a connecting corridor leads to the chapel gallery in the choir of the Franciscan Church.

History of the building: Very little is known about the mediaeval bishops' residence, and the first verifiable details date from the alterations made by Wolf Dietrich. At his behest were built, shortly before 1600, the wing on the Residenzplatz and Domplatz, with the Carabinierisaal, the section linking up with the Franciscan Church, with the western arcades bridging the Franziskanergasse, and also a quadrangle to the north of the Franciscan Church, with the garden "Dietrichsruh" in the centre. Of this there still remains the south wing, built on to the church, with fine stucco ceilings. Archbishop Marcus Sitticus had the north wings of the building constructed, and they were completed under Paris Lodron. In 1660, a third storey was added, with attic. Archbishop Hieronymus Colloredo (1772—1803) planned to renovate the entire western part; but of this project, which would have included the demolition of the nave of the Franciscan Church, only the quadrangle of the "Toscana Wing" was realised.

*The Residenz Gallery,
portrait of Cardinal
Matthäus Lang, c. 1520*

THE RESIDENZ GALLERY

This is the successor to the archiepiscopal collection of paintings which Hieronymus Colloredo had assembled in 1789 from the estates of the various episcopal palaces. In the mid-18th century, the collection comprised about 1000 paintings. The dissolution of the ecclesiastical principality in 1803 caused the
collections to be dispersed, and in 1806/09, when Salzburg belonged for the first
time to Austria, the most valuable of the works, including paintings by Lukas
Cranach, Hans Baldung Grien, Rueland Frueauf and Konrad Laib, were taken
to Vienna. The occupation by the French (1809) and the Bavarians (1810—1815)
hastened the disintegration of the collections, and in 1816, an auction dispersed
the modest remains. In 1923, the gallery was founded anew, with works from
the "Czernin" and "Schönborn-Buchheim" collections. Acquisitions and re-
purchases of items of the former collection have made the Residenz Gallery
once more an important collection of paintings of the 16th-19th centuries. The
Gallery is accommodated in the third storey of the Residenz.

The Franciscan Church

After the Cathedral precincts and St. Peter's Monastery, the Franciscan Church, as the parish church of "Our Dear Lady", is the third ecclesiastical centre of the town. To visit this church is to travel through the history of art in Salzburg. The best idea is to enter by the west portal in the Sigmund-Haffner-Gasse, which leads into the Romanesque nave with its triple aisle. The side aisles are dark and vaulted, the main aisle narrow and almost without any independent source of daylight. A narrow and very high triumphal arch opens the view on to a bright Gothic choir, the extent and height of which can, from the nave, only be surmised. The widest contrasts become apparent: whereas the late Romanesque nave (1223) with its solid walls and pillars, its weighty vaults and dividing bays, still gives a feeling of straitness and confinement, the eye rejoices in the bright spaciousness of the late Gothic hall choir (1st half of the 15th century), which has an atmosphere of width and freedom. The slender round pillars seem to grow aloft like tree-trunks, the intricate network of the rib vaulting stretches overhead like a lattice of branches. The outer walls are pierced by great traceried windows; breadth and light dominate in this hall, expressing new religious life. The baroque era (17th century) saw the building of the chapels between the interior buttresses; the high altar was designed by Fischer von Erlach in 1708.

History of the building: The history of this church is extremely complicated and has not yet been entirely elucidated. In the 8th century, there stood on this site a baptistery (belonging to St. Peter's) which Bishop Virgil had renovated. In 1139, this old church was separated from the monastery and assigned to the canons as a parish church. It had been besides, since 1130, the convent church of the nuns of St. Peter's, for whom an area in the back part of the nave was reserved until 1458. Since 1592, after the dissolution of the convent, it has been also the church of the Franciscan monastery.

Consecration of the new building is mentioned in 1223, and its late Romanesque nave is still preserved. It is probable that the old church building was damaged in the town fire of 1167, and that the new one was begun at the end of the 12th century. This late Romanesque new building is not uniform; between the side and the main aisles, various phases in the building process are evident from the south portal and from the capitals of the embedded columns. The form in which the choir terminated is unknown, although a non-projecting transept is probable. The building of the choir should perhaps be seen in relation to the very slow rebuilding of the cathedral; it is possible that a choir was built here soon after the devastating fire of 1167, to offer a temporary substitute for the cathedral. The Gothic era: In 1408 it was decided to build a hall-church, and Hans von Burghausen was engaged as master builder. In 1422 the eastern parts of this late Gothic church were under construction, in accordance with the first design, which allowed for six bays. But there was a change of plan, probably before 1432 (death of Hans von Burghausen): it was decided to erect the eastern part as an independent section in the style of a central hall, but using the old nave. The ribbed vaulting was now designed as a central theme, the west bay became a connecting bay, and the triumphal arch was erected in 1446. The old

Romanesque south portal was also rebuilt with substantial alterations — higher (through the insertion of Gothic corbels under the lintel) and wider. The old archivolt stones had to be modified for use over the wider portal. The radial butt-joints were worked obliquely outwards, resulting in a slightly "lobate" contour, due to the smaller radius of the archivolt stones. This re-use of the old portal bears out other such retardative, "Romanising", tendencies found in Salzburg in the 15th century.

A first consecration of the altar is reported in 1449, and the choir was completed in 1460 by Stefan Krumenauer. The tower was erected in 1486—1498 to a design from Nuremberg. The neo-Gothic spire dates from the year 1866. Complete restoration of the interior and exterior was carried out in 1983/84.

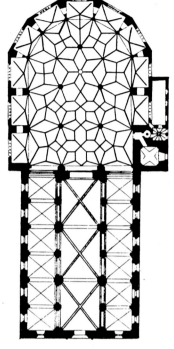

Interior: The chiaroscuro contrast was originally not so pronounced; before the oratories were built in above the side aisles (1450 and 1592), the main aisle received plenty of direct daylight through the clerestory windows; up to 1600 the choir, too, had more — though darker (stained-glass) — window area, with the windows which were then obstructed by the building of the Residenz. So the present chiaroscuro effect is the result of the alterations of the baroque period, the time of chiaroscuro painting. The marked spatial contrast, however, existed from the beginning, and was deliberately employed as a stylistic feature in the 15th century.

Decoration and furnishings: The high altar, designed in 1708 by Johann Bernhard Fischer von Erlach, dominates and enhances the chancel, standing like a small circular temple beneath the central pillar of the choir, and emphasising its centrality. The centrepiece of the altar, framed by the guardians of the shrine, SS. George and Florian (sculptures by Simeon Fries), is the late Gothic miraculous image of the Virgin Mary, by Michael Pacher. Along with the head of the Child (rediscovered in 1983), and several panels (now in the Austrian Gallery in

The Franciscan Church, view of the Gothic hall-choir

Vienna) it is a relic of the former Gothic altar by Michael Pacher, probably his principal work. Pacher worked on it in Salzburg from 1484 until his death in 1498. The Christchild is an impersonal, academic 19th century creation. Thomas Reckeisen constructed the fine wrought-iron altar-screen in 1780.

The ring of chapels: In the niches between the buttresses of the choir are chapels which show the progress of style throughout the 17th century. In the first north bay is the oratory of Archbishop Wolf Dietrich, erected in 1606, perhaps to plans by Vicenzo Scamozzi, in the style of a secular palace façade.
1. (from NW to NE) Chapel of Archbishop Marcus Sitticus, dedicated in 1610 to St. Karl Borromäus.
2. Chapel of the Birth of Christ, installed by Archbishop Wolf Dietrich in 1600; the altar painting is attributed to Francesco Vanni.
3. St. Roch's Chapel, donated by the town in 1625, the year of the plague.
4. Chapel of the Holy Cross, 1670.
5. Deep choir chapel with marble altar by Hans Asslinger (1561) from the old cathedral. Stucco-work c.1700, painting (1670) by Wilhelm Faistenberger.
6. (from SE to SW) Chapel of St. Joseph, 1704, painting by Friedrich Pereth.
7. St. Sebastian's Chapel, c.1700, painting attributed to Francesco da Siena.
8. St. Anne's Chapel, Kuenburg family vault; stuccoed in 1680 by Paolo Brenno, paintings by Christoph Lederwasch.
9. St. Francis' Chapel, 1693, Thun family vault; stucco by Ottavio Mosto, excellent painting by Michael Rottmayr.
In the side aisles of the nave, late 19th century altars; neo-Romanesque front of the choirloft from the same period.

In the west wall of the south aisle is embedded the plain gravestone of St. Virgil (Sanctus Virgilius), made of red Adnet marble.

This slab came from the saint's tomb, erected by Archbishop Wichard in the old cathedral. The inscription reads: "In the year of Our Lord 1315 on 26th September, Archbishop Wichard of Salzburg interred here the body of St. Virgil". In 1598/99, during the demolition of the old cathedral, this tomb was also destroyed; the saint's remains and this stone arrived by a circuitous route in the Franciscan Church in 1612. When the Cathedral was consecrated in 1628, the relics were transferred back there, but the tombstone remained here in the Franciscan Church.

On the triumphal arch there are vestiges of Gothic frescoes from the workshop of Konrad Laib: on the left, a Christ in Agony above a Eucharist shrine which was installed in front of the temporary dividing wall during the alterations in 1446; on the right, the Virgin Mary with saints, and scene on the Mount of Olives, dated 1447. In the archway to the choir is the late Gothic pulpit, the steps up to which are guarded by a lion being stabbed by a man in armour (taken over from the Romanesque building).
South portal: Romanesque portal in the Lombardic style, presumably from two early phases of building (late 12th century and beginning of the 13th century); the present height and width date from alterations in the first half of the 15th

century (cf. history of the building). The tympanum relief shows Christ between SS. Peter and Rupert. The inscription reads: "Guide, O Shepherd, the herd Thou dost cherish. May the merit of St. Rupert soothe Thy spirit. As this work of art shines forth in glory, even so may God adorn inwardly the purified heart." The west portal, also originally Romanesque, was probably given its present form around 1700, when the west façade was fashioned to suit the taste of the age.

THE FRANCISCAN MONASTERY

The modest buildings of the Franciscan Monastery are in the Franziskanergasse, opposite the nave of the parish church. A marble relief of St. Francis, dating from 1605, crowns the former main portal of the monastery, which is linked with the Franciscan Church by a covered bridge. This was built in 1592, when Archbishop Wolf Dietrich allotted the parish church as the monastery church to the order of mendicant friars, after he had taken over, in 1583, the convent of the disbanded nuns of St. Peter's.

The Monastery of St. Peter   ④

The precincts of St. Peter's Monastery extend from the Small Festival Hall in the west to the Kapitelplatz in the east, and from the Mönchsberg rock to the Franziskanergasse. The main entrance is in the Franziskanergasse, opposite the tower of the parish church.

The outer courtyard is overshadowed by the high precipice of the Mönchsberg, and the grey stone tower of the monastery church soars aloft in emulation of this rock face. Art and nature confront each other; the tower is crowned in rich baroque style, the green patina of the roof vying with the tree-tops on the cliff. The portal to the right of St. Peter's Church leads into the ancient cemetery of St. Peter. This shady refuge directly beneath the precipice may well have been the cradle for the infancy of the town. For it was here, in the shelter of the natural caves in the conglomerate rock, that — even before the arrival of St. Rupert in 696 — a community of monks may have sought a retreat, where they survived the troubles of the Great Migrations. The beginnings of this community are lost in the mists of history, but it is possible that it was already in existence at the time of St. Severin (mid-5th century). Later centuries have preserved the memory of this beginning in the rock by reading significantly from the name of Rupert that very "rock" (Lat. rupes=rock) on which he founded Salzburg's church and dedicated it to St. Peter. Thanks to its established origins in the late 7th century, St. Peter's is considered to be the oldest monastery still extant in the German-speaking world.

The monastery precincts of St. Peter's

THE COURTYARDS

The entire layout of the monastery consists of three courtyards surrounded by buildings. The easternmost courtyard, to the north of the church, is part of the cloister and is not accessible to visitors; remains of the old cloisters are preserved here, on the site of the oldest monastery buildings. The outermost courtyard, with the Fountain of St. Peter, by Bartholomäus Opstal (erected in 1673), dates back to alterations made by the great 18th century abbot Beda Seeauer (1753–1785). Two passages in the west wing lead to the Collegium Benedictinum, built in 1926 to plans by the Berlin architect Peter Behrens (1868–1940). The frescoes on the façade were executed in 1925 by the Salzburg artist Anton Faistauer (1887–1930). In the part between the two passages, a room is fitted out as a **memorial to Michael Haydn** (1737–1806), with autograph scores and personal belongings of this musician whose life and work were closely bound up with the monastery.

THE MONASTERY CHURCH

The main part of this church — the only Romanesque one preserved in Salzburg — is simple in outline, consisting of clear-cut, cubic forms. Only the baroque dome over the crossing and the complex structure of the steeple stand out in effective contrast, softening with their sweeping contours, which have less to do with geometry than with music, the austerity of the architectonic expression. This expression of architecture still persisted in Salzburg, old-fashioned and severe, true to "Romanesque" forms, when elsewhere Gothic cathedrals were already springing up. The "Romanesque" tower and the vestibule with its bulky rib vaulting was built in 1400 — no obligation was felt towards the new trends; it was more important to continue the old traditions.

The interior of the church, too, preserves, beneath the splendid late baroque attire that covers the walls like a fine web, the severity of the Romanesque building. One substantial change, however, was brought about by the baroque lighting. In the narrow, windowless centre aisle, the eye is directed upwards to the brightly lit vaulted roof which, above the shading cornice, collects all the daylight from the deep-set windows in its vaults. The dome over the crossing brings the intensification and the culmination of this lighting, which gives the magical effect of a sphere of light over the heads of the faithful. This interior is characterised by light and colour, by ethereal ornamentation and spaciousness.

Decoration and furnishings: The decoration of the monastery church is particularly rich, with splendour accumulated over the centuries. The portal of the vestibule and its tympanum were built in the incipient classical style; the sculptures of the Christchild and of the Apostles Peter and Paul are the work of Franz Hitzl (1781) and the statue of St. Rupert is by J. Anton Pfaffinger (1756). Displayed in the vestibule are Roman funeral chests (containers for urns) which were found under the floor of the church. Under these chests is a stone block with vine ornamentation, which could have been a part of the decoration of the early Carolingian Amandus Chapel.

The Romanesque church portal: Like the south portal of the Franciscan church, this is a recessed portal in the Lombardic style, from the early 13th century. It, too, bears witness to various phases of alteration, the Roman arch under the lintel, for instance, being a later addition. The tympanum relief shows Christ flanked by Peter and Paul; the Latin inscription reads: "I am the gate of life, come all ye in need of healing, enter by me. There is no other way that leads to life." Through the Romanesque portal one enters the tower hall, adjoined on the right by the Chapel of the Holy Spirit and on the left by St. Wolfgang's Chapel. The great screen is a masterpiece by the court ironsmith Thomas Hinterseer (1768).

From the **Romanesque basilica,** built in 1130, the Hildesheim system of 2 columns alternating with 1 pillar is still readily recognisable, as well as the raised transept. The Romanesque base of the westernmost pillar of the north wall (directly to the left of the entrance) was laid bare, and the fourth column of the north wall shows the original Romanesque marbling. The rood altar occupied the last bay before the crossing, and in the north and south side aisles are preserved some frescoed remains of the ornamentation of this rood screen, dating from the second half of the 12th century. The walls of the main aisle under the former raftered ceiling were frescoed, and a remnant of this 12th century painting is discernible on the south wall, in the bay before the crossing.

After a first phase of baroque innovation, which had already at the beginning of the 17th century encroached upon the Romanesque substance by the erection of the dome, the vaulting of the centre aisle and the demolition of the apses, the church was remodelled, under Abbot Beda Seeauer, in uniform rococo style. The delicate rocaille stucco was the work of Benedikt Zöpf, the marble altars were executed by J.N. Högler to designs by Lorenz Härmbler.

The ceiling frescoes in the nave represent scenes from the life of St. Peter; they are, like the paintings in the dome showing the Eight Beatitudes and the Doctors of the Church, the work of the Augsburg artist Johann Weiss.

The decoration of the walls of the main aisle in the manner of a picture gallery also harks back to the first "baroque" phase at the start of the 17th century. The great painting on the south wall, by Kaspar Memberger (1591), shows Christ carrying the cross, and comes from the old cathedral. The "Elevation of the Cross", on the north wall, by Ignazio Solari (son of the cathedral architect) is dated 1632. Around 1660, the next two paintings, by Thiemo Sing, were added: in the northern one, St. Benedict is blessing King Totila, in the southern one, Rupert is showing Theodo, Duke of Bavaria, the newly-founded monastery. Under Abbot Beda, Franz Xaver König painted the series of St. Benedict and St. Rupert pictures in the upper row on the north and south walls respectively. Almost all the altar paintings are the work of the Krems artist Johann Martin Schmidt (1718—1801), who painted about 30 pictures for the monastery.

The altars: North wall from W to E: Apostle altar, "Christ teaching the Apostles", by J. M. Schmidt; centre altar, "Death of St. Benedict", by J. M. Schmidt; Angel altar, "Guardian angel", by Reslfeld (1704).

South wall from W to E: Scapular altar, "Gift of a scapular to St. Simon", by J. M. Schmidt; centre altar, "Death of St. Rupert", by S. Paur (1661); Joseph altar, "The Holy Family" by J. M. Schmidt.

Altars in the side chapels of the south aisle, from W to E (all paintings by J. M. Schmidt): "The 14 Votive Saints venerating the Eucharist"; St. Theresa altar, "Vision of St. Theresa"; "The Immaculate Virgin Mary"; "Pietà"; "Worship of the Lamb of the Apocalypse".

Transept altars, paintings by J. M. Schmidt: north altar, "Beheading of John the Baptist"; south altar, "Glory of St. Vitalis".

The painting on the high altar, with SS. Peter, Paul and Benedict before the Virgin Mary, was also the work of J. M. Schmidt (1778).

The Monastery Church of St. Peter

Noteworthy among the remaining furnishings is "Maria-Säul", a "Schöne Madonna" from about 1420, with baroque gilding, in the north transept. In the south transept is one of the most important works of late Gothic tombstone sculpture in Salzburg, the gravestone of St. Vitalis, by Meister Johannes (1497). In the south aisle, at the back of St. Rupert's altar, lies sunk into the ground the "rocky grave" of St. Rupert. A Roman sarcophagus is the coffin, and the slab, dating from 1444, bears the slightly raised image of the saint. The superstructure by Simon Baldauff, with sculptures by J. G. Hitzl and paintings by Fackler, was completed in 1741.

In the 15th century, a row of chapels was built on to the south side aisle. In the first chapel from the west stands the tomb of Hans Werner von Raitenau, the father of Archbishop Wolf Dietrich, sculptured in 1593 by Veit Eschay. The magnificent bronze-cast candlesticks, donated by Wolf Dietrich, are also attributed to Eschay. In the chapel opposite the tomb of St. Rupert are the memorial for Michael Haydn (by Anton Högler, erected in 1821) and the plaque for Marianne von Berchtold zu Sonnenburg (W. A. Mozart's sister, "Nannerl"). The great organ in the west gallery still has the old casing by Lorenz Härmbler, who re-used in 1763 sculptures by Hans Waldburger from 1624.

Early history of the monastery precincts: The early history of the development of the monastery buildings is still uncertain. The latest research seems to indicate that the new foundation of the monastery by St. Rupert in 696 is to be found in the area of the Cathedral; indeed, it would seem that the origins of St. Peter's are really bound up with the cathedral and its monastery. Excavations underneath St. Peter's Church have not been able to ascertain any absolutely identifiable monumental church building before the year 1000, but this is not yet the last word on the matter. The main churches were built, in the 11th and 12th centuries successively, around the so-called "two-chamber building", as around a *locus sacer;* there are also fragments of Carolingian stones with interlace decoration, and the early Carolingian stone block in the vestibule, originating from the monastery precincts. The impression is that a major building was erected *after* 987, when the estates of the cathedral monastery were separated from St. Peter's. On the other hand, it is conceivable that there was a number of smaller churches or chapels in the area of St Peter's, similar to a Carolingian "family of churches". In the Encomia of Alcuin, various chapels are named, and moreover, the explicit designation of canons and monks in early sources supports the view that there existed a secluded monastic community. The former dedication to St. Patrick of St. Gertrude's Chapel in the "catacombs" also indicates a very early use of the caves within the framework of monastic life. It must be assumed that in the early period (8th—10th century) there existed a family of churches, with the cathedral and its canons' quarters at the centre, but that the monks of this community were accommodated around the chapels by the Mönchsberg cliff. It was not until the separation — also economic — of the community of monks from that of canons in 987, that St. Peter's blossomed as an autonomous centre. In the 11th century, a large basilica was built, with west tower, choir crypt and side aisles terminating in apses. Then the 12th century brought the building erected under Abbot Balderich (1125—1147), and substantial parts of this are still recognisable today.

St. Peter's Cemetery, on the right the "catacombs" in the rock

St. Gertrude's Chapel in the Mönchsberg rock

ST. PETER'S CEMETERY

The peculiar charm of this place always manages to draw the visitor under its spell. A visit to the so-called "catacombs", the cave chapels in the Mönchsberg rock, is to be recommended without fail. The entrance is on the right of the Chapel of the Holy Cross in the first arcade in the rock. (Times of guided tours are displayed here.)

The "Catacombs": Going up the steps from the communal vault, one comes to the Chapel of St. Gertrude. It was originally dedicated to St. Patrick (†461), the patron saint of Ireland, and in 1178 Archbishop Konrad III added a dedication to Thomas à Becket, murdered eight years previously. The rock face is divided into six arched niches, and remnants of frescoes show the martyrdom of Thomas à Becket. Further steps lead up to the Maximus Chapel. On the right is an *arcosolium* (bench-like tomb) with an inscribed plaque dated 1521, relating the legend of a martyr. It is conceivable that this "martyr's grave" in the style of an early Christian *arcosolium* represents a historic fiction of the Salzburg

Humanist prior and Abbot of St. Peter's, Kilian Püttricher. Worthy of note is also a triple apse with a horseshoe-shaped ground plan, hewn in the rock.

The Chapel of the Holy Cross: The small chapel beside the entrance to the "catacombs" was established in 1170 as a family vault. In the rock, opposite the entrance, is "St. Rupert's prayer cave" (so called since the 17th century), with a remarkable immense perforated block of gypsum in a niche in the rock. (The nearest incidence of this mineral is in Kuchl.) The St. Aegidius Chapel, which has over the altar a Gothic fresco from 1430, is reached by a small staircase which was moved here at the beginning of the 17th century when Paris Lodron, then still a canon, started making baroque-style alterations to the Holy Cross Chapel, intending it as his burial chapel.

The St. Catherine or Mariazell Chapel: This was built on to the south transept of the church in 1227, donated by the Babenberg Duke Leopold VI of Austria. The apse still shows the original Romanesque structure; the interior was stuccoed in 1792.

St. Margaret's Chapel: This was built in 1485—1491 in the middle of the cemetery on the site of the old Amandus Chapel. On the walls, both exterior and interior, many splendid late Gothic gravestones are preserved.

The row of arcades screening the cemetery from the bustle of the town was erected in 1626, after the cathedral cemetery was demolished and room had to be made for the graves of prominent citizens.

Leaving St. Peter's Cemetery towards the Kapitelplatz, one suddenly hears the sound of rushing water; this is the Almkanal gushing out of the mountain. The tunnel through the Mönchsberg for this freshwater stream is a major engineering feat of the 12th century.

Hohensalzburg Fortress ⑤

A visit here is an essential part of the programme; the outlook affords an impress-ive panorama of the town and the mountain ranges. From the station in the Festungsgasse, next to the exit from St. Peter's Cemetery, one takes the funicular (Festungsbahn) up to the "Hasengraben" bastion.

The fortified wall is the prime characteristic of this fortress, in which large, flat, enclosed areas dominate. The towers are subordinate in importance to the walls, and occupy only the corners. These walls rise out of the forest like smooth cliffs reshaped by human hand into fortifications. Hohensalzburg is not a knight's castle in the romantic style, with turrets, battlements and frivolous balconies; no tales of "white ladies" haunt these walls. On the contrary, the fortress was until 1800 a quite prosaic functional construction, repeatedly altered to suit the latest techniques of warfare. It was always the focus of political events, so life there was too busy for ghosts.

Clearly visible from the bastions are the old fortifications on the Kapuzinerberg opposite, a reminder of Archbishop Paris Lodron's fortification of the town during the Thirty Years' War. The most extensive bastions, with trenches, demi-lunes and curtains, were in the Mirabell area, the most vulnerable part of Salz-burg. The gates of the town were dedicated to various saints, for "where 'tis not God that guards the city tower, in vain is all the watchman's might and power". The picturesque castle ward with linden tree, cistern and St. George's Church, and the castle museum may be visited without a guide; the state rooms, which are amongst the finest secular Gothic rooms in Europe, may be visited only on a guided tour.

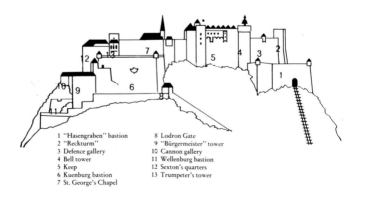

1 "Hasengraben" bastion	8 Lodron Gate
2 "Reckturm"	9 "Bürgermeister" tower
3 Defence gallery	10 Cannon gallery
4 Bell tower	11 Wellenburg bastion
5 Keep	12 Sexton's quarters
6 Kuenburg bastion	13 Trumpeter's tower
7 St. George's Chapel	

North side of the Hohensalzburg Fortress

The "Goldene Stube" in the Hohensalzburg Fortress

The interior of the fortress, as it appears today, dates primarily from the construction carried out under Archbishop Leonhard von Keutschach (1495—1519), and his coat of arms with the turnip is to be found all over the place. The Church of St. George was altered in 1501, at his behest, to late Gothic, with marble reliefs of Christ and the Twelve Apostles ornamenting the interior. On the outside of the chapel, the Leonhard von Keutschach Memorial from the year 1515, attributed to Hans Valkenauer, has found its second home.

The Fortress museum: This is installed in the "Hoher Stock", the castle keep, extended and furnished by Archbishop Leonhard. Old weapons, guild insignia, objects of cultural and historical value and mementos of Archbishop Wolf Dietrich are exhibited here. The "Rainer Museum", which occupies the rooms in which Wolf Dietrich was kept prisoner after his overthrow, contains equipment from the infantry regiment no. 59, "Erzherzog Rainer", in existence since 1682.

Ward in the Fortress, with cistern and St. George's Chapel

The state rooms: These constitute the only still extant late Gothic sovereign residence. They were installed by Archbishop Leonhard in the fourth storey of the "Hoher Stock". Richly carved marble portals lead from the entrance hall into the "Goldener Saal", where walls and roof are studded with gilded wooden ornamentation; a frieze of coats of arms decorates the roof beam, and massive marble columns with twisted stems support the ceiling by the north wall, which faces towards the town and was formerly open. The "Goldene Stube" is even more richly ornamented. Intricate late Gothic gilt and coloured foliage carving is rampant around the doors, Gothic tracery forms a variety of friezes, carved rosettes enliven the originally leather-covered walls. The *pièce de résistance* is the tiled stove dating from 1501, one of the most magnificent examples of late Gothic tiling. The guided tour also includes the so-called "Salzburger Stier" (Stier = bull) in the wooden shed above the Kuenburg bastion. It is a set of flue-pipes tuned to an F major triad, and is the only surviving Gothic "Hornwerk". Its strident F-A-C chord (fac! = Latin imperative of "do") gave the command for the opening of the town gates in the morning and their closing in the evening. In the 16th century, the "bellow" was supplemented by a mechanical barrel organ. Between Palm Sunday and 31st October, the "bull" can be heard in the town at 7 a.m., 11 a.m. and 6 p.m., immediately after the Glockenspiel.

Brief history of the building: Theodo, Duke of Bavaria, presented to St. Rupert in 696, along with the town of Salzburg, the "Obere Burg" — meaning the settlement on the Nonnberg terrace and the actual fortress rock, which was probably partly walled round. During the investiture struggle, there was erected, under Archbishop Gebhard (1060—1088), a strong fortification which was extended under Konrad I (1106—1147). The greatest extension took place in the 15th century, in the late Gothic period, under Archbishop Leonhard. The interior of the fortress has remained since then substantially unaltered. Paris Lodron had barriers and bastions added in the 17th century, and the great Kuenburg bastion, built in 1681, to the north of St. George's Church, was the last extensive piece of building.

The Kaiviertel and Nonntal districts

THE NONNBERG CONVENT

The Convent of St. Erentrudis is the oldest existing convent in the German-speaking world. St. Rupert founded it in 712/15 in the "Obere Burg" (the settlement up on the Nonnberg terrace), and installed his niece Erentrudis as the first abbess. The modest convent buildings and the late Gothic basilica with its west tower dominate the Nonnberg to the east of the Fortress. By way of the Festungsgasse and the Höhenweg, the convent can be reached on foot in 10 minutes from the Kapitelplatz. One goes through the small cemetery south of the church to arrive at the main portal, which was built in 1497—1499 in the late Gothic style, using the old late Romanesque tympanum and foliated lintel. The tympanum (c. 1210) shows the Virgin Mary flanked by John the Baptist and St. Erentrudis on the right, and by an angel and a kneeling nun on the left. The Latin inscription reads: "Reflected glory, image of the Father, fecund womb, gateway, light, source; faith in the birth of the Saviour".

Apart from the choir of the Franciscan Church and the Church of St. Blasius, the convent church is the only Gothic building of any notable size in Salzburg. In comparison with them, however, it gives an impression of antiquity due to its basilican ground plan with raised choir and choir crypt, which form a clear link with the previous Romanesque building. The choir of nuns is partitioned off in the rear part of the nave; in the northern side aisle, an oratory with "Romanesque-type" columns was added in 1570. Despite the archaisms in both ground plan and elevation, the decoration follows the style of the period around

Crypt of the Nonnberg Convent Church

1500. Reticulate rib-vaulting, traceried friezes and screens, and ogee arches with crockets adorn the surfaces. With the variety of profiles of the clustered pillars, the interior appears to be bounded by "trellises", the areas in between being either frescoed or closed in by stained-glass windows. The late Gothic crypt under the choir, with the tomb of St. Erentrudis, is most impressive. The rib vaulting spreads out, supported by 18 columns.

Decoration and furnishings: Remaining from the Romanesque decoration of around 1150 are frescoes in the niches of the former vestibule below the nuns' choir-loft; they show the figures of saints, and are of exceedingly high artistic quality. One can identify SS. Augustine, Benedict and Gregory, as well as deacons.

The centre window of the choir was donated in 1480 by the aristocratic Klanner family of Salzburg and executed by Peter Hemmel von Andlau, from Alsace. The high altar, a fine late Gothic winged altar dating from 1515, was brought here in the 19th century from the church of Scheffau. In the shrine are the Virgin Mary and SS. Rupert and Virgil; in the altar crowning is the Cucifixion. The wings bear on the inside scenes in relief-work of the Passion of Christ, and on the outside tempera paintings after Albrecht Dürer's series of woodcuts representing the life of the Virgin Mary. The altar in the south transept is the work of Meister Wenzel (1522), and on the north transept altar is a Pietà from around 1420. The simple, elegant pulpit (1475) bears the coat of arms of the Abbess Agathe von Haunsperg.

History of the building: St. Rupert founded the Convent and the Church of Our Lady in 712/715. Rebuilding was begun in about 1000, and the Emperor Heinrich II and his Empress Kunigunde are said to have been present at the consecration in 1009. The consecration of the crypt may have taken place in 1024 or 1043. The church was decorated with frescoes in the mid-12th century. In 1423, church and convent were destroyed by fire. In 1463—1471, Meister Sigmund had charge of rebuilding the choir and the crypt, and the nave was built by Wolfgang Wiesinger from Braunau in 1484—1505.

From the Nonnberg convent, one can either take the Höhenweg back to the Kapitelplatz, walk down the steps of the Nonnbergstiege to St. Cajetan's Church, or go through the south fortified gateway to Nonntal and the Church of St. Erhard.

ST. ERHARD'S CHURCH

In the façade of St. Erhard's, architectural elements from the most varied sources combine to form a charming whole. The plain, unecclesiastical-looking windowed front, framed by narrow risalites, suddenly becomes effective through the addition of a projecting marble pediment supported by four slim columns; the high tambour dome makes clear the overall significance, and, along with the towers, gives the church its ecclesiatical look. The interior is a central hall which has three separate apses and of which the dome is the cardinal feature. The Italian Giovanni Gaspare Zuccalli built this church at the behest of Archbishop Max Gandolf, in 1685—1689. The stucco was the work of Carlantonio and Francesco Brenno; in the spandrels of the dome are the figures of SS. Rupert, Virgil, Vitalis and Martin. The high altar was donated in 1692 by Archbishop Johann Ernst Thun, with sculpture by Andreas Götzinger and painting by Johann Michael Rottmayr: "St. Erhard baptising the pagan princess Ottilie".

Background history: St. Erhard's, dedicated to the patron saint of the sick, and mentioned in documents in 1310 and 1404, belonged to the Nonnberg convent and was the chapel of the small convent hospital. In 1603, Archbishop Wolf Dietrich acquired it as the hospital chapel for those employed in the cathedral chapter. The Gothic church, because of its delapidated state, was demolished, and Zuccalli's building was consecrated in 1689.

ST. CAJETAN'S CHURCH

It is dedicated to SS. Cajetan and Maximilian, and was the monastery church of the Theatine monks from 1700 until the dissolution of the Order in 1809. This building by Gaspare Zuccalli, erected in 1685—1700, is characterised by the contrast between the mighty oval tambour dome and the broad palatial façade. Church and monastery together form a single unit, the church being simply a

The suburb of Nonntal with St. Erhard's Church

part of this, distinguished on the exterior by the dome and the pediment. The volute gables on colossal pilasters on either side emphasise the impression of a stage flat given by this façade. The church interior is a broad oval, completely dominated by the cupola, the four cross-arms giving the effect of annexed chapels.

Decoration and furnishings: The stucco-work, sparing in comparison with that in St. Erhard's, is the work of the Brenno brothers. Paul Troger painted the dome fresco in 1727/28, this being his first major commission for such a work; the theme is the Holy Trinity, the Virgin Mary making intercession, and the heavenly hosts. Also by Troger are the paintings on the high altar: "The Martyrdom of St. Maximilian" (1727), and on the right-hand side altar: "The Apotheosis of St. Cajetan" (1735). Johann Michael Rottmayr painted in 1708 the "Holy Family" on the left-hand side altar. The angels on the high altar are the work of the Salzburg sculptor Matthias Wilhelm Weissenkirchner, from the years before 1727. The interior was restored in 1982. Through the left portal, one comes to the "Holy Staircase", a copy of the 28-step "Scala Sancta" in the Lateran Palace, the "Pilate" stairway up which Christ was led, and which is supposed to have been brought to Rome by Helena, mother of Constantine the Great; this staircase may be ascended only upon the knees. Archbishop Franz Anton Fürst ordered its incorporation in 1712. In the side-chapels are altar paintings by Jakob Zanussi, notably "St. Sixtus" (1733).

The "Bürgerstadt" (Burghers' Town)   ⑥

Huddled at the north side of the systematically planned Ecclesiastical Town is the Burghers' Town with its narrow streets. Rows of houses and the Church of St. Michael border the Residenzplatz, and the projecting archway beside the church leads through to the Waagplatz, the old centre of the burghers' quarter. Here, adjacent to the church and the archway (the "porta"), stood the imperial palace of the Bavarian dukes of the Agilolfing family; this was the residence of Duke Theodo's son Theodbert (c. 680–after 716) and his son Hucbert. The ducal palace was linked with the ecclesiastical fort around the cathedral by the "porta", whose passage is still used today. The tradespeople settled around this gateway and had markets there, and the tribunal was held in a loggia built on to the north wall of the church, until it was moved into the first town hall (Waagplatz no.1) in 1328.

ST. MICHAEL'S CHURCH

This little church, dedicated to the Archangel Michael, stands on ancient soil; it was the palatine chapel of the dukes, and the parish church of the burghers who lived in the area of the palace. Owing to alterations carried out in the 17th century, its present form goes back primarily to the baroque trend under Abbott Beda Seeauer in the latter half of the 18th century. The church has retained the chapel-like dimensions of its early days; looking from the Mozartplatz towards the Residenz and the Cathedral, one can hardly imagine a greater contrast. St. Michael's, with its delicate tower more like a ridge-turret, calls to mind smaller-scale settlements or even villages. Whereas the Cathedral precincts were built on a generous scale, the ecclesiastical and secular power of the princes being given palpable expression in splendid architectural style, St. Michael's still bears witness to the days when the Archbishop of Salzburg was not yet a prince, and was opposed by secular power in the person of the duke palatine.

Decoration and furnishings: This "chamber" church with its narrowed square choir was renovated in baroque style under Abbott Beda Seeauer in 1767–1773. St. Michael's belongs to the monastery of St. Peter, so that some of the craftsmen who took part in the alterations to the monastery church also worked here. The stucco (1769) is by Benedict Zöpf, the screen (1770) by Philipp Hinterseer. The ceiling frescoes with angel choirs and the Archangel Michael are attributed to Franz Nikolaus Streicher. Franz Xaver König did the paintings on the side altars, and the high altar painting, dating from the first phase of the alterations, is reputed to be the work of Tobias Bock (c. 1650).

History of the building: The imperial Agilolfing palace was already here at the time of Rupert (around 700). Archbishop Arno renovated the Church of St. Michael, which was then rebuilt under Adalram (821–826). The "porta" is first mentioned in 930, and the church became the responsibility of St. Peter's in 987. After the great fire of 1167, the palace was completely rebuilt, and St. Michael's was reconstructed as a "tribune" church. On the ground floor stood the altar of St. Nicholas, patron saint of the tradespeople, and in the tribune was the altar of St. Michael, guardian saint of the gateway chapels. In 1291, Archbishop Konrad IV demolished the city tower and the porta, the remains of the imperial palace of Barbarossa. Gothic windows were inserted in 1383, and in 1496 Michael Pacher painted panels for St. Michael's altar in the tribune. In 1617—1620, a sacristy was built on to the south side, the church was vaulted, the tribune pulled down and the St. Michael altar by Pacher moved to the presbytery. A great deal of baroque rebuilding was carried out under Abbott Beda Seeauer in 1767—1773, when the tower and the vaulting were renewed.

THE ROMANISCHER KELLER (Romanesque cellar)

The entrance is in the house at no. 4, Waagplatz, immediately on the left after the archway; the cellar lends atmosphere to the exhibitions held here. This room, with its great round pillars and massive capitals, is left over from the imperial palace built in 1167; over it stood the palace (today no. 7, Residenzplatz and no. 4, Waagplatz), from the first floor of which the gallery of the palatine Chapel of St. Michael could be entered.

THE MOZART MONUMENT

On a marble pedestal showing the emblems of the various categories of music stands the larger-than-life bronze statue of Wolfgang Amadeus Mozart. Ludwig Schwanthaler from Munich won the commission in 1839, over his competitor Bartolini from Florence, and the monument was erected in 1842. It has a cool, academic look, less reminiscent of Mozart's music than of a heroic musical figure.
The courtyard of the house at no. 4, Mozartplatz (the former Andretter house) is worth a visit; one is surprised by the miniature dimensions of an 18th century private chapel with a charming façade.

THE GEORG TRAKL MEMORIAL

On the Waagplatz stands the "Trakl house" (no. 1a), the birthplace of the poet Georg Trakl (1887—1914); autographs and mementos of the poet are displayed in the room where he was born.

ALTER MARKT (the old market place)   ⑦

Entering one of Salzburg's oldest streets, the Judengasse, we pass the "Höllbräu" inn, where until 1404 the synagogue stood, and continue along to the Alter Markt. In the course of the town's expansion, the main market was moved here from the Waagplatz in about 1300. In the centre still stands the old fountain with the figure of St. Florian (who affords protection against dreaded outbreaks of fire), made in 1734 by Josef Anton Pfaffinger. The basin of the fountain is fine stonemason's work of 1687, and the wrought-iron scrollwork railing was taken over at the time from the previous fountain of 1585. At the upper end of the

The "Alter Markt" with the St. Florian fountain

market place is the Café Tomaselli, founded in 1703 and rich in tradition, a favourite meeting-place. Opposite is the "Hofapotheke", court pharmacy of the prince-archbishops, with the original rococo fittings from around 1760.
The Alter Markt is surrounded on three sides by burghers' houses; the façades are late 18th and early 19th century. These houses are sparingly decorated; they are distinguished by genteel discretion. This is a general feature of bourgeois architecture in Salzburg: there are no oriels, no superabundant ornamentation; the houses have a modest air. The façades are topped by a cornice, and behind the parapets are concealed the divided ridged roofs (in profile, a flattish repeated V) — there are no steep roofs in Salzburg.
A glimpse into the organisation of the old Salzburg bourgeoisie is afforded by the Rathaus (town hall) on the Kranzlmarkt, at the beginning of the Getreidegasse; the town council was moved here from the Waagplatz in 1407. One would be unlikely to find such a small, modest town hall in any comparable town; here is once more that discretion of architectural form. (If one compares the puny little tower with the other towers in the town, it is obvious who called the tune here!) At the beginning of the 17th century, it underwent alterations, and the figure of Justice, by Hans Waldburger, over the entrance, belongs to this period (1617).
The **Getreidegasse** ("corn lane") is one of the oldest thoroughfares in Salzburg. This narrow gully of a street has retained its mediaeval character. The gateways lead into courtyards with several storeys of arcades, connected by passages to the parallel streets. There are many fine shop signs preserved from the 18th and 19th centuries.

MOZART'S BIRTHPLACE   ⑧

Wolfgang Amadeus Mozart was born on 27th January, 1756, in the house at Getreidegasse no. 9. His father, Leopold, was *kapellmeister* at the archiepiscopal court. The family's apartment was on the third floor. In the small museum are displayed portraits of Mozart and his family, his half-size violin, his full-size violin and his "Hammerklavier" (piano). On this floor are also newly-opened rooms showing a middle-class apartment typical in Salzburg in W. A. Mozart's day. On the second floor is the exhibition entitled "Mozart on the Theatre".

THE BÜRGERSPITAL CHURCH OF ST. BLASIUS   ⑨

This church is built against the Mönchsberg cliff at the end of the Getreidegasse. The plain Gothic architecture is in the tradition of the mendicant orders. The lack of a tower was intentional, the small ridge-turret being sufficient for the purposes of a hospital chapel. The interior of this hall-church is just as unpretentious as its exterior, effective through its very clarity and simplicity of line. The cross rib vaulting above the octagonal pillars divides the nave into seven bays. In the west part of the church, a gallery for the sick was added in the 15th century.

The birthplace of Wolfgang Amadeus Mozart in the Getreidegasse

Decoration and furnishings: Still preserved from the Gothic furnishings is the fine "Holy Sepulchre" (1481), erected to the left of the high altar, on the gospel side. This delicate shrine in the form of a Gothic church was designed to represent for the faithful the tomb of Christ. The high altar (1785) is in the classical style, the painting on the Altar of the Epiphany in the south nave is the work of Paul Troger (1746), and the figures of John the Baptist and John the Apostle are by Josef Anton Pfaffinger.

History of the building: Hospital and church were founded in 1327, the church consecrated in 1350. In order to facilitate attendance at Mass for the sick, a gallery was built into the west part in 1428; it is linked to the "Gothic hall" and the hospital buildings, and there used to be an altar of St. Elizabeth in it. The crucifixion scene on the exterior was added in the 19th century, and the traceried windows date from the days of Gothic revival. The relief of St. Sebastian on the north side, created by Konrad Asper in 1614—1620, once adorned the Linzer Gate.

In the **Bürgerspital** (burghers' hospital), which still retains its 16th century form, the Toy Museum (Spielzeugmuseum) is installed, with items from the collection of the Folk family. On the ground floor, there are also show-rooms belonging to the Museum Carolino Augusteum.

The Festival precinct   ⑩

This area of the town, between the Bürgerspital and the Monastery of St. Peter, had been for centuries open farming land and gardens. Archbishop Wolf Dietrich had the court stables for 130 horses built here, against the Mönchsberg cliff, by the quarries. In the mid-17th century, the stables were extended by buildings for a riding-school, and during the years 1695—1732, three archbishops made systematic alterations and additions.

HOFMARSTALL AND PFERDESCHWEMME (court stables and ornamental horse-pond)

The court stables, more like a palace than an outbuilding for horses, and the sumptuous ornamental pond for washing these noble beasts emphasise the great importance of the horse as a symbol of princely rank and prestige in the baroque age. Monarch and realm, ruler and subjects saw themselves mirrored allegorically in the image of the horse and the horse-breaker or trainer. Alexander the Great and his war-horse Bucephalus were the ideal of harmony between rider and steed; wise government was equated with this harmony, breaking in and training with perception and discrimination, "without blows or spurs".
Johann Bernhard Fischer von Erlach designed the façade in 1693, with its grand

The Large Festival Hall and the ornamental horse-pond

portal on which a frieze of arms, atlantes and unicorns with the personifications of Europe and Asia are a reminder of the glorious part played by a contingent of Salzburg cavalry in the battle against the Turks in 1683. The ornamental pond, rebuilt in this form in 1732 by the supervisor of the court gardens, Franz Anton Danreiter, represents the dramatically exaggerated apotheosis of the horse. The group with horse and tamer, which was only then raised and turned to face the front, is framed by the central motif of the triumphal arch in the "backdrop" wall. The fresco in the arch shows the embodying in a constellation of the winged horse Pegasus, and the fall of Bellerophon is a warning against losing one's sense of proportion. The horse pictures on the ornamental wall portray the different temperaments of the various breeds of horses.

THE LARGE AND THE SMALL FESTIVAL HALLS

There is a guided tour including both halls. The Small Festival Hall was built in 1926 to designs by Clemens Holzmeister; the frescoes in the foyer (1926) are by Anton Faistauer. The plans for the Large Festival Hall were drawn up in 1956; Clemens Holzmeister moved the enormous stage into the Mönchsberg rock, so that the former stables could be retained as the foyer. The Latin inscription along the main frontage reads: "The sacred home of the Muses stands open to lovers of art, so that divine power may bear us in rapture heavenwards".

Since 1926, the former summer riding-school, the "Felsenreitschule", with its rows of arcades hewn out of the Mönchsberg rock face, has been used as a theatre. It was roofed over in the course of alterations in 1968—70. The adjacent winter riding-school, with its enormous ceiling painting of a "Türkenstechen" ("Turk-sticking") by Johann Michael Rottmayr and Christoph Lederwasch (1690), serves as a foyer.

History of the building: The exercise-ground in the "Frauengarten" is mentioned for the first time in 1593, and in 1606, Archbishop Wolf Dietrich erected his court stables here. Archbishop Guidobald Thun added the winter riding-school in 1662. Then Archbishop Johann Ernst Thun carried out extensions and provided a horse-pond. Johann Bernhard Fischer von Erlach designed the façade of the stable and the horse-pond in front (1693/94); the group with horse and tamer is a major work of the sculptor Bernhard Michael Mandl (1695), the grand portal is by the stonemason Wolf Weissenkirchner. The modification of the Felsenreitschule (1693) also goes back to designs by Fischer. Under Archbishop Leopold Anton Firmian, the horse-pond was remodelled in 1732 to plans by Danreiter; the basin, balustrades, "backdrop" wall and pedestal of the horse with tamer all date from that year. Josef Ebner painted the horse frescoes, and only the statue by Bernhard Michael Mandl was taken over from the previous construction.

The building complex opposite the Festival Halls housed the Benedictine university founded by Archbishop Paris Lodron in 1622. In 1810, after the brief annexation of Salzburg to Bavaria, it was dissolved, to be revived in 1850 as a faculty of theology; it was re-established as a state university in 1962. The quadrangle of buildings accommodates today the library, the great hall and various institutes of the University.

THE NEUTOR (new gate)

The Neutor or Siegmundstor is a tunnel bored through the narrowest part of the Mönchsberg in 1764 by the engineer Elias von Geyer at the behest of Archbishop Sigismund Schrattenbach. The brothers Wolfgang and Johann Baptist Hagenauer were responsible for the decoration of the portals (1767). On the portal facing the town is mounted a medallion portraying Archbishop Sigismund, with the inscription: "Te saxa loquuntur" (The rock celebrates you). Over the Riedenburg portal is an exceptionally fine statue of St. Sigismund. The entrance is flanked by two broken obelisks; here, too, stood the Hagenauer brothers' "Ruinenbastei", an arrangement of ruins intended as a reminder of the former Juvavum (Roman Salzburg).

In the Hofstallgasse, opposite the Festival Halls, stands the **"Wilder-Mann-Brunnen".** This fountain was erected by the municipality in 1620 on the bank of the Salzach, as a container for live fish. The "Wild man", something between a river god and a satyr, has been tamed here into a guard and escutcheon-bearer of the town.

The narrow building diagonally opposite the Small Festival Hall houses the **Rupertinum Graphic Art Collection,** where special exhibitions are held of 19th and 20th century European art.

The **Langenhof,** the building opposite the Collegiate Church, is one of the few aristocratic palaces in Salzburg. Archbishop Max Gandolf Kuenburg had it built for his family in 1670, and the façade was renovated around 1800. In a wall-niche in the main entrance (Sigmund-Haffner-Gasse no. 16) stands a great Romanesque lion dating from the early 13th century. The Latin inscription reads: "This sculpture was chiselled under the care and supervision of Brother Bertram. May God unite him with the Blessed." The lion, which certainly came from the demolished Romanesque cathedral, once bore a column on its back.

THE COLLEGIATE CHURCH   ⑪

This was founded in 1694 as the university church, and dedicated in 1707 to the Immaculate Virgin Mary. It is a masterpiece by Johann Bernhard Fischer von Erlach and a major work of the European baroque period. Great cubic forms are piled up, culminating in a steeply-rising dome. The façade, to the north, is unusual, indeed unique, and without precedent in the history of architecture. The mighty central section swells out to present an entrance of broad arcades. Colossal pilasters, a high centre window extending up into the entablature, and high oval windows lend emphasis to the vertical line, which culminates in a sweeping diadem with the figure of the Immaculata. The towers, which give a visual impression of independent, almost free-standing elements, flank the central section, and move in so close that they seem to squeeze it into prominence. High, narrow Roman windows and the individualistic crowning structure with volutes, balustrades and sculptures remove any suspicion of clumsiness by making the towers seem lofty.

The Interior: The interior of this cross-in-square church with central cupola is unexpectedly lofty. The colossal pilasters begin high above floor-level, so that one moves around amid giant pedestals; this gives the impression of an inaccessibly high space. It has an atmosphere of clear and austere spirituality, as befits a university church. Only in the choir does an irrational element take over, in the form of an angel-populated nimbus around the Immaculata. Two enormous free-standing columns, an allusion to the temple of Solomon, comprise the distinctive feature of the presbytery. In the angles between the arms of the cross are four oval chapels, dedicated to the four patron saints of the university faculties.

The Collegiate Church on the University Square

Decoration and furnishings: On top of the towers stand the four Evangelists and the Doctors of the Church, works of the sculptor Michael Bernhard Mandl. The sculptures in the niches along the nave were executed in 1904 by J. Piger. The tabernacle, which replaces a *tempietto* by Fischer, was made to a design of 1738—1740 by Johann Kleber. The fine stucco, notably that of the angel nimbus, was the work of Diego Francesco Carlone and Paolo d'Allio. The side altars were not installed until 1725-1727, with sculptures by Josef Anton Pfaffinger and altar paintings (on the right St. Benedict, on the left St. Karl Borromäus) by Johann Michael Rottmayr (1721/22). There were plans for dome and ceiling paintings by Rottmayr, abandoned, however, for reasons unknown. The faculty chapels: the altars were made by the court carpenter, Simon Anton Baldauff (1721—1724), and the sculptures came from the workshops of Josef Anton Pfaffinger and Meinrad Guggenbichler (1721/22). SE chapel: Thomas Aquinas (Theology), painting by Johann Georg Bergmüller. SW chapel: St. Ivo (Jurisprudence), painting by Franz Georg Hermann, 1722. NW chapel: St. Catherine (Philosophy), painting by J. G. Bergmüller. NE chapel: St. Luke (Medicine), altar painting from Admont. South of the presbytery adjoins the Chapel of the Holy Cross; the pulpit was built in 1774. Restoration of the exterior in 1984/85 with the original white/grey colour-scheme.

Gstättenviertel ⑫

This quarter of the town takes its name from the romantic Gstättengasse, the narrow street beginning at the Inneres Gstättentor, beside the Bürgerspital Church, and leading along the foot of the cliff to the Klausentor. On the Anton-Neumayr-Platz are Salzburg's two largest museums — the **Natural History Museum** (Haus der Natur) and the **Museum Carolino Augusteum,** which houses collections from prehistoric times right up to the 20th century. To mention but a few of the most important exhibits: the Celtic bronze "beak-jug of Dürrnberg" by Hallein is a masterpiece of toreutic art from about 400 B.C. In the entrance hall are displayed parts of the monument made of red Adnet marble to adorn the imperial tombs in the Cathedral of Speyer. Emperor Maximilian I had commissioned this rotunda from Hans Valkenauer, but owing to the deaths of both men, 1519, it remained unfinished. In the stairway hangs a fine Romanesque tympanum portraying the Virgin Mary, dating from around 1200; this could well have come from the old cathedral.

The "Haus der Natur" is a natural history museum with a difference. By means of an "Outer Space" room, aquarium, terrarium and dioramas, the phenomena of nature are attractively and instructively made comprehensible to visitors.

THE SATTLER PANORAMA

From the Anton-Neumayr-Platz, a lift takes one up on to the Mönchsberg. There, in the reception hall of the Café Winkler, is displayed the "Sattler Panorama". This panoramic view, 26 x 5 metres, reproduces the view from the For tress in the year 1825. Three painters worked on it: the buildings are by Johann Michael Sattler (1786—1847), the landscape by Friedrich Loos (1797—1890) and the figures by Johann Josef Schindler (1777—1836).

From here, it is a pleasant walk over the Mönchsberg to the suburb of Mülln On the way, it is worth going by the "Humboldt - Terrasse". This natural terrace in the rock offers an impressive view of the town; it was named after the famous traveller Alexander von Humboldt, who wrote after a visit to Salzburg: "The regions of Salzburg, Naples and Constantinople are in my opinion the most beautiful on earth."

ST. MARK'S CHURCH (the former Ursuline Church)

In 1695, Archbishop Johann Ernst Thun founded an educational establishment for girls, under the administration of the Ursuline nuns. The church, dedicated to St. Mark, was built in 1699—1705 to plans by Johann Bernhard Fischer von Erlach; the convent buildings were not completed until 1726. Fischer thought of a highly original plan for fitting the church into the site at the end of the nar row open space by the Klausentor; to accentuate the perspective of the church with the streets forking back on either side and the lineal continuity of the con vent buildings, he moved the towers behind the façade, thus jointing the church as it were, to the complex of the convent. Pilasters, entablature and pediment form a strict division of the façade, the wall area being further minimised by large doorways and windows. The slim, column-like, low-roofed towers have an Ital ianate look, and crowning the pediment are statues of SS. Ursula, Mark and Au gustine. The interior is a very richly stuccoed hall with a rudimentary transept the point of intersection marked by a windowless saucer-dome. This dome and the vaulting are decorated with paintings by Christoph Anton Mayr (1756) "God the Father in his Glory" and "Christ and the Virgin Mary receiving St Ursula". Renovation and restoration of the building, which had been in a severe state of disrepair, was completed in 1980.

MÜLLN CHURCH

The Church of St. Mary in the suburb of Mülln is an architectural landmark at the north-west approach to the town. The Gothic nave with its steep roof and the tower with its baroque lantern characterise the unmistakable outline. A co vered staircase with chapels overcomes the problem of difference in height and leads to the inside of the church. Baroque alterations were carried out on this Gothic "chamber" church, partly in the 17th century and then to a greater ex tent in the 18th century; Christoph Fenninger executed the involute Régence style stucco-work in 1735—1738.

St. Mark's Church in the Gstättenviertel

Decoration and furnishings: The painting on the Holy Trinity Altar in the upper stair-case chapel is the work of Johann Martin Schmidt (1769). The high altar, erected in 1758—1760 to a design by Vinzenz Fischer, bears the mid-15th century miraculous image of a Madonna with Child. The side chapels were added to the nave in 1605—1610 by the brothers of Archbishop Wolf Dietrich. The altar painting in the first chapel on the left, "Christ appearing to St. John in St. Facundo", is attributed to Johann Michael Rottmayr (c. 1690). In the first chapel on the right is Rottmayr's "Virgin Mary with Child, venerated by SS. Augustine, Nicholas Tolentinus and Clara", and stucco dating back to Wolf Dietrich. The second chapel on the right is the tower chapel. The Hagenauer brothers designed this fine altar in 1765; it is modelled on Fischer von Erlach's altar in the Francis-can Church, and has as its centrepiece a copy of the miraculous image of Genazzano. The second chapel on the left is dedicated to St. Nicholas Tolentinus, with the altar painting "St. Nicholas Tolentinus with St. Paul the Hermit and St. Anthony", by J. M. Rottmayr (1690); the stucco dates from the Wolf Dietrich period. The pulpit is the work of Johann Georg Hitzel (1738).

History of the building: The Gothic building was erected, starting in 1439, on the site of an old chapel of St. Mary, and was consecrated in 1453. Above the wooden baroque vaulting, the Gothic reticular rib vaulting is still preserved. The design of this church, with its partitioning interior buttresses, points to Peter Harperger as the architect. In 1461/65, Mülln became an independent parish, and a collegiate foundation was built for the community of canons (the complex of buildings to the NW of the church). The Au-gustinian Hermits took over the parish in 1605, and chapels were added to the church. The baroque lantern on the tower dates from 1673, the outer façade of the staircase, the stucco by Diego Francesco Carlone in the sacristy and the complete baroque modifica-tion from 1705. In 1835, the Order of Augustinian Hermits was dissolved, and the parish became the responsibility of the Benedictine monastery of Michaelbeuern.

ST. JOHN'S HOSPITAL CHURCH

A 15-minute walk from Mülln takes the visitor to the fourth Salzburg church designed by Fischer von Erlach, which stands in the grounds of the Landeskran-kenanstalten (general hospital). Archbishop Johann Ernst Thun founded the church with a hospital (the wings on either side); the foundation stone was laid in 1699, and the consecration was celebrated in 1704. The façade, which in its simple style harmonises with the hospital wings, demonstrates once again Fischer's partiality for dominating pilasters with wall areas merely inserted. The interior is tastefully and uniformly decorated, with concave corners and a rudi-mentary transept with a quadripartite vault in the centre. A vault is sunk under the raised altar with its round tabernacle. The side altars bear paintings by Johann Michael Rottmayr: the "Beheading of St. Barbara" and the "Sermon of John the Baptist" (1709).

THE NEW TOWN

The district on the right bank of the Salzach has retained its small-town character; it developed from the settlement at the bridgehead of the Salzach bridge (now Staatsbrücke) at the convergence of the important main roads from Linz (Linzergasse) and the Salzkammergut (Steingasse). Like the Bishops' Town, this quarter was also walled round for the first time in the 13th century, and a protective stronghold was built — the "Trompeterschlössl" (c. 1300), the present Capuchin monastery. Small-scale industry and artisans settled here; inns and hostelries offered shelter to travellers. Outside the walls to the west, gardens stretched down to the Salzach. Archbishop Wolf Dietrich had his summer residence, "Altenau" — the present Mirabell Palace — built here in this garden landscape in front of the city gates. Two decades later, Paris Lodron included the palace and gardens in his extended ring of fortifications; however, building in this area was still sparse, and the Mirabell district remained the "front garden", so to speak, of the Bishops' Town. It was not until Paris Lodron's fortifications were sacrificed to the demands of Modernism in the last third of the 19th century, that somewhat random building began — and has unfortunately persisted until today.

HOLY TRINITY CHURCH   ⑭

The complex of buildings comprising the Priests' House and Holy Trinity Church in the Makartplatz is, next to the Mirabell Palace and Garden, the main architectural feature of the New Town. Archbishop Johann Ernst Thun founded the Priests' House (for seminarists) and the Collegium Virgilianum (a hostel which enabled indigent aristocratic and middle-class youths to pursue their studies) in 1694, and commissioned Johann Bernhard Fischer von Erlach to draw up the plans. Holy Trinity Church was consecrated in 1702, and was Fischer's first church building in Salzburg. His design is along the lines of a monastery; to the left of the church was the accommodation for the seminarists, to the right the Collegium Virgilianum.

The modern observer easily misses the connexion between the church and the hostel buildings, for the high towers over-emphasise the church façade. The towers were originally quite different; in place of the bell turrets with clock and windows, the main cornices were topped simply by flattish roofs rather like those of the Collegiate Church towers (but without sculptures and balustrades). Thus the dome had the full effect of a sole imposing motif, and the integration of the façade in the Priests' House was more clearly visible. Gaspare Zuccalli's lateral oval dome on St. Cajetan's Church rises more abruptly; Fischer integrated the oblong oval dome of Holy Trinity Church more strongly into the façade, enhancing the effect with pairs of massive columns, which look from a distance as if they support the dome, and with the concave façade, curving in towards the dome and forming a lateral oval with the flight of steps and the landing in front. The sculptures crowning the columns (personifications of Faith, Hope, Love and the Church) are the work of Michael Bernhard Mandl (1699).

The dome extends over the whole interior, and the oblong oval hall gives a constricting impression. The altars stand in the narrow cross-arms. The interior is restrained, the drum downright sober — as befits the church of a seminary and a school.

Decoration and furnishings: The fresco in the dome, by Johann Michael Rottmayr (1697) shows the crowning of the Virgin Mary by the Holy Trinity. Into the sections above the niches were fitted pictures of the Doctors of the Church (also by Rottmayr), but these were destroyed in the great fire of 1818. These additional paintings lent more colour to the interior. The high altar, completely altered in 1843, was reconstructed in 1955 using the original parts, but Fischer's heart-shaped tabernacle could not be traced. The angels on the side altars are the work of Michael Berhard Mandl (1700—1702). In the mid-18th century, the town pawnshop was put up in front of Holy Trinity Church — this was the first occasion for raising the towers, in 1757; after the great fire of 1818, Wolfgang Hagenauer raised them once more and gave them their present shape.

Holy Trinity Church on the Makartplatz

Reconstruction of the façade with the towers in their original form (F. Fuhrmann)

MOZART'S DWELLING-HOUSE

From 1773, the Mozart family lived at no. 8, Makartplatz, in the so-called "Tanzmeisterhaus". This is where Wolfgang Amadeus Mozart wrote all the compositions belonging to his last years in Salzburg — over 150 works. The living quarters were destroyed by a bomb in the Second World War; the "Tanzmeistersaal" was fortunately preserved, and today makes a charming setting for concerts.

Diagonally opposite, at the corner of the Makartplatz, stands the Landestheater, a building from the highly productive "theatre factory" of the architects Hermann Helmer and Ferdinand Fellner, erected in 1892 on the site of Paris Lodron's former ballrooms. Close by, at no. 26, Schwarzstrasse, is the home of the International Mozarteum Foundation, built by the Munich architect Richard Berndl in 1910—1914. The Mozarteum is the starting-point for the guided tours of Mozart's house and the "Zauberflötenhäuschen" (the "Magic Flute" hut), which is set up in the bastion garden behind the Mozarteum. Wolfgang Amadeus Mozart is said to have composed the "Magic Flute" in this summerhouse in 1791, in Vienna; Salzburg acquired it as a gift in 1875.

The Mirabell Palace and Gardens   ⑮

The Palace and its grounds have developed over more than three centuries. Around 1610, Archbishop Wolf Dietrich had the garden palace "Altenau" built here for his mistress, Salome Alt; his episcopal successors extended it to make the archiepiscopal summer residence, the Mirabell Palace. Immediately upon his accession, Archbishop Johann Ernst Thun commissioned Johann Bernhard Fischer von Erlach with the remodelling of the gardens. Under Ernst Thun's successor, Franz Anton Harrach, Fischer's greatest rival, Johann Lukas von Hildebrandt, took over the supervision. The fire of 1818 destroyed much of the palace's former splendour, and it was reconstructed in the dry manner of a municipal building.

On the Makartplatz, beside the Landestheater, is the entrance to the Mirabell Gardens. Stone fencers on high pedestals form a gateway, and gods of classical antiquity, in Alpine guise, jostle on the balustrade. Round the basin of the fountain in the parterre are groups of figures involved in intensive activity — dramatic rescue, deathly struggle, abduction; perched on heaps of rock, they are indifferent to the bustle of the gardens around them. To the left of the entrance, Hercules lifts the giant Antaeus up from the earth, high into the air, and crushes him; further forward on the left, towards the Palace, a sinister king bears off a struggling woman; this is Pluto, lord of the Underworld, abducting Proserpina to his dark realm. He enticed her into coming near by causing a huge and wondrously

The Mirabell Gardens with the Palace in the background

beautiful flower to grow in his garden. During her sojourn in the Underworld, vegetation on earth dies, but as soon as she comes up to spend other half of the year with her mother, springtime awakes the plants to life again. Foremost, on the right, Paris carries off Helen, the loveliest of women, and flees with her over the sea to Troy. In revenge, the Greeks destroy his native town, and only Aeneas can save himself, his aged father Anchises and his son Ascanius from burning Troy — this is the group at right front. The rape of Helen and the rescue of Aeneas take place with the help of Venus, the goddess of love; secluded gardens are her favourite place. Hercules, on the other hand, is a model for the virtue of the prince who, "strong in heart", overcomes vice in the shape of the son of the earth-goddess. Elemental and earthly forces are at work in the garden; the Olympian gods on the balustrade at the entrance observe these proceedings from a

The marble staircase in the Mirabell Palace

distance. The four groups are also, however, mythical representations of the four elements air, earth, water and fire — of the various, constantly changing mixtures of which all matter was thought to be composed. These sculptures were executed in 1690 by Ottavio Mosto. The low building and the small courtyard on the right of the parterre belonged to the orangery; they housed the orange-trees in winter. One wing accommodates the **Salzburg Baroque Museum,** which evolved from the Rossacher Collection; on exhibition here is European art of the 17th and 18th centuries — primarily oil sketches, designs and *bozetti* for altar paintings and frescoes.

In front of the Palace, a balustrade with fine stone vases encloses the modern rose-garden. This was once the orange orchard, with over 500 small orange trees growing in it during the summer.

The main parterre, from the Palace to the entrance, looking over to the Old Town and the Cathedral, dates back to the plans drawn up by Johann Bernhard Fischer von Erlach in the period around 1688. The main axis is the backbone of the layout of every baroque garden, starting from the loggia of the palace or castle. This ideal has not been realised in the Mirabell. The re-shaping had to be based on the Manneristic early baroque layout, in which the Palace was situated asymmetrically in relation to the main axes, and the garden consisted of a number of small, individually-planned contiguous gardens. This diversity of the parterres in the Mirabell gardens has remained, despite all the remodelling.

The narrow parterre to the south of the Palace, with the Pegasus fountain and the avenue running parallel to the main parterre, is of more recent date, and the result of bourgeois garden-planning. The copper Pegasus (forged in c. 1660 by Maximilian Röckh after a design by the Innsbruck court sculptor, Caspar Gras) was placed here in 1913, after extensive peregrinations through the squares of Salzburg. The pair of lions and the pair of unicorns which now guard the steps accompanied Pegasus for a time, as the heraldic beasts of the Thun family. Going up the "unicorn"steps (built in 1894), one arrives at the aviary with its trellised cupola; it was erected in about 1700, and is now used for exhibitions. The small staircase between the lions leads up to the bastion with the "Zwergl-garten" (Zwerg = dwarf). Archbishop Franz Anton Harrach had these little monstrosities made shortly after his accession in 1709; the Bavarian Crown Prince Ludwig had them removed in 1812, and their present arrangement is not original.

Turning left before the bridge, one comes to the "Heckentheater" (Hecke = hedge) of 1717, one of the earliest of its kind in the German-speaking world. There is a stage and an orchestra pit, with the clipped hedges arranged to from wings and backstage. The Heckentheater is a last vestige of Matthias Diesel's re-shaping of the garden under the supervision of Johann Lukas von Hildebrandt. The "Susanna fountain" at the end of the avenue in the small parterre dates from about 1610, and was probably taken over from the garden of Wolf Dietrich's Altenau.

THE PALACE

This square, four-winged building, which no longer looks much like a summer residence, was given its present form after the great fire of 1818. A model of the old palace is displayed in the vestibule.

In the years 1721—1727, Johann Lukas von Hildebrandt combined the individual old parts of the building to form a homogeneous palace. Remaining from this period are the vestibule, the staircase, the great hall and the chapel. The staircase, aside from the main axis and too narrow, does not conform to the baroque ideal; Hildebrandt had to take into account the distribution of space in the previous building — but he nevertheless achieved a charming result. A vital element of its individuality is the rich, ebullient ornamentation of the staircase. The laborious business of climbing stairs suddenly becomes fun, when accompanied by the billowing movement of the stone waves with cherubs sporting on their crests. One is borne along, so to speak, on the upsurge of the tide. The walls of the stairway are punctuated with niches in which bucolic figures posture. The banister and the statues in the niches are the work of Georg Raphael Donner (1726); the ceiling fresco by Bartholomeo Altomonte and Gaetano Fanti (1723) was destroyed in the fire of 1818.

The Marmorsaal (marble hall): The fire destroyed the ceiling fresco in this room, too, but the rest of the magnificent decoration has been preserved in its original form. Gilt and coloured artificial marble give an air of splendour, and the walls are covered with filigree patterns. Foliation, cartouches, cornices and pilasters create a strict pattern in which apparent licence of form is curbed by symmetry.

The chapel, accessible from the Mirabellplatz, was dedicated in 1726 to St. Nepomuk. Here, too, the ceiling fresco (by Bartholomeo Altomonte, 1725) was destroyed. The fine marble high altar was erected in 1722.

History of the building: We have little idea of how the summer residence of Altenau-Mirabell looked in the 17th century. The first baroque modifications date back to Johann Bernhard Fischer von Erlach, who had been engaged in the task since 1687/88. The main parterre with the "Four Elements" by Ottavio Mosto (1690), the orange orchard with the stone vases and most of the gods on the balustrade date from this period. The gods are (at the entrance): Chronos, Bacchus, Jupiter, Mars, Hercules, Vulcan, Mercury, Apollo and (bordering the garden) Diana, Flora, Minerva, Ceres, Pomona, Venus, Vesta and Juno — all the work of Bartholomäus Opstal and Johann Frölich, except Flora, Ceres, Pomona and Vesta, the personifications of the four seasons, which are by Mosto. The present arrangement is probably not in accordance with Fischer's intention; they may perhaps have been originally designed for the large groups around the central fountain. With the accession of Franz Anton Harrach in 1709 came Hildebrandt's first contributions. The loggia, the *sala terrena*, was added in 1713, probably together with the small parterre, which had a row of six arbours with fountains. (The *sala terrena* between the palace and the aviary was demolished in 1818; the flight of steps was built in its place in 1894.) The

Heckentheater and the plans for a Zwerglgarten date back to the period when Matthias Diesel was inspector of the court gardens, from 1713 to 1717. Hildebrandt's alterations to the palace were carried out in 1721—1727. Johann Kleber stuccoed the vestibule in 1736. In 1791, the dismantling of the tower was planned, since classicism endeavoured to achieve a uniform architecture composed of regular blocks. The fire of 1818 in the New Town had also severely damaged the Mirabell; the reconstruction and the modification in classical style were carried out by Peter de Nobile to plans by Johann Georg Hagenauer. Until 1824, there was in front of the main façade of the Palace, on the Mirabellplatz, an ornamental horse-pond with Pegasus, lions and unicorns (now in the Garden), erected in 1704.

St. Sebastian's Church

St. Sebastian's, in the Linzer Gasse, was the chapel of the municipal old people's home. Kassian Singer built this baroque church (1749—1754) on the site of a previous late Gothic building (1505—1515). The great fire of 1818 destroyed Paul Troger's frescoes and high altar painting, and to a great extent the furnishings, also. Fine workmanship is displayed in the main portal in the Linzer Gasse, executed by Josef Anton Pfaffinger to a design by Franz Anton Danreiter. Of the original furnishings, the screen by Philipp Hinterseer (1752) deserves special mention. On the high altar now stands a Madonna with Child, by Hans Waldburger, c. 1610.

The tomb of Paracelsus: In the passage between church and cemetery is the tomb of Paracelsus, erected here in 1752 using the original gravestone. Philippus Aureolus Theophrastus Bombastus von Hohenheim (1493—1541) was a famous physician and scientist. He did much to revolutionise chemistry, pursued original researches, and saw the main purpose of chemistry in preparing and purifying medicaments. He enriched the science of chemistry by the "tria prima" — sulphur, mercury and salt, being the three basic elements of the body of man.

THE CEMETERY

The destruction of the cathedral cemetery under Archbishop Wolf Dietrich necessitated a new graveyard within the town boundary. The Archbishop had the old cemetery of St. Sebastian extended and bordered with arcades in 1595—1600 by Andrea Bartoletti, in the form of an Italian *campo santo*. In the centre, he erected his mausoleum, dedicated to the Archangel Gabriel. Graves from all centuries are preserved in the arcades.

The atmosphere of St. Sebastian's cemetery is essentially different from that of St. Peter's. In the latter, nature still dominates the graveyard in spite of all the buildings, the natural terrain is preserved and the closeness to nature has a soothing effect. In St. Sebastian's, on the other hand, the strict proportions of the architecture set the tone. The deep arcades are paved with marble, and massive marble altars enhance the overall impression of rigidity and petrifaction.

The mausoleum of Archbishop Wolf Dietrich in St. Sebastian's Cemetery

THE GABRIEL CHAPEL

This magnificent building, whose tiled walls are unique in Western Christian architecture, was designed by Elia Castello. The chapel was erected in 1597—1603 as a mausoleum for Archbishop Wolf Dietrich, and the sarcophagus of this prince, whose influence on Salzburg was so decisive, is in the vault. The decoration with coloured glazed ceramic tiles is said to have been carried out at the behest of the Archbishop; the tiles were made by Hans Khop. Wolf Dietrich's idea for this kind of decoration may have derived from the Spanish mode of ornamentation with *azulejos*. In the wall-niches stand larger-than-life figures of the four Evangelists, and the barrel-vault of the altar niche portrays in coloured stucco the four Cardinal Virtues and the Doctors of the Church. The dome stretches, tent-like, over eight golden acanthi with busts of angels, Wolf Dietrich's coat of arms linking them at the apex of the dome. Mounted on the walls on either side of the altar niche are bronze memorial plaques, cast by Christoph Herold, from Nuremberg, in 1605 and 1607. The inscriptions describe the building of the chapel (left-hand plaque) and give instructions for Wolf Dietrich's burial by night without pomp and circumstance (right-hand plaque).

The grave of the Mozart family: On the way to the mausoleum, one can see, on the left after the arcade, the grave of Wolfgang Amadeus Mozart's widow, Konstanze von Nissen (†1842). Wolfgang's father, Leopold (†1787), is also buried here, as well as Konstanze's second husband, Nikolaus von Nissen (†1826), and her aunt, Genoveva von Weber (†1789), the mother of Carl Maria von Weber.

The Kapuzinerberg ⑰

THE KAPUZINERKLOSTER (Capuchin monastery)

In the Linzer Gasse no. 14, at the great rustic portal with its relief of St. Francis, begins the Stefan-Zweig-Weg up the Kapuzinerberg. Six rustic Stations of the Cross (c. 1740) line the way. Beautifully situated at the edge of the wood is the Paschingerschlössl, where the writer Stefan Zweig lived from 1919 until 1934. The Capuchin monastery was built in 1599—1602 by Archbishop Wolf Dietrich, on the site of the "Trompeterschlössl", which is mentioned as early as 1291. The monastery church is, in accordance with the rule of the order, a simple hall frugally furnished. The late Gothic church door (1450) with the busts of prophets carved in it is said to have come from the old cathedral. The side altars were erected in 1700—1702; the painting on the high altar, representing the Birth of Christ, was donated by Wolf Dietrich.
The bastions below the monastery are well worth a visit; the so-called "Kanzel" (pulpit) affords a wonderful panoramic view of the town.

THE FRANZISKISCHLÖSSL

In 1629, during the Thirty Years' War, Paris Lodron caused the Kapuzinerberg, too, to be fortified all round with walls and bastions. The Franziskischlössl at the top of the hill served as quarters for the guards. It can be reached on foot in about 20 minutes, by a path through the wood, starting at the gate above the monastery. The fortified building has remained practically unaltered; a pleasant outdoor café has been installed in the courtyard.

THE CHURCH OF ST. JOHANN AM IMBERG

Taking the romantic Imbergstiege (Imberg staircase) back down to the town from the monastery, one passes the tiny Church of St. John, first mentioned in documents dated 1319. Archbishop Max Gandolf had it renovated in 1681, and its present decoration and furnishings date from the 18th century. The Imbergstiege comes out in the **Steingasse;** it is worth turning left, away from the town, and walking along here through the Inneres Steintor.

The narrow old Steingasse was one of the main traffic arteries of the New Town. It had to be constructed right at the foot of the cliff, since the unregulated Salzach extended to the south side of the houses. From the "Äusserer Stein", the end of the Steingasse, with the "Engelwirt" fountain on which Archbishop Ernst Thun's heraldic beasts, the lion and the unicorn, embrace each other, it is not far to Schloss Arenberg, at no. 10, Arenbergstrasse. Here lived Hermann Bahr, from 1912—1922; the villa now houses a Max Reinhardt Memorial Research Centre. Special exhibitions are held here during the Salzburg Festival.

The Palace and Gardens of Hellbrunn

The Palace of Hellbrunn lies about 5 km. to the south of Salzburg, at the end of the Hellbrunner Allee, which starts by Schloss Freisaal, in Nonntal. In the 15th century, there were already episcopal fish ponds and a zoological garden on the well-watered Hellbrunner Berg. Archbishop Marcus Sitticus, Graf von Hohenems, (1612—1619) chose this district for his country villa; building was begun in the spring following his accession, and the palace and gardens were completed in essentials two years later (1613—1615). The chief architect was most probably the cathedral designer Santino Solari, and the work was carried out partly by Salzburg artists, but mostly by Italians who, like Solari, came from the Intelvi Valley by Lake Como.

The major importance of Hellbrunn lies in the preservation, practically unadulterated, of the original state of this Manneristic early baroque palace with its park and gardens. Whereas most Manneristic gardens were altered completely during the baroque period, Hellbrunn has to a great extent managed to retain its distinctive character.

The Palace and Gardens of Hellbrunn

Marcus Sitticus, Wolf Dietrich's cousin, had, like his uncle, been brought up in Italy, and took with him to Salzburg the idea of the Italian *villa suburbana*. His model for Hellbrunn was not, however, the Roman villas of his uncle, Cardinal Marco Sittico Altemps, but the style of the Venetian villa on the Terra Ferma. The difference is apparent principally in the use of water in the landscaping. The palace and gardens of Hellbrunn are laid out on a level, like the Venetian villas; the water flows in quiet rivulets or spouts in thin jets. In the Roman villas of Frascati or Tivoli, on the other hand, streams rush through the gardens covering the mountain slopes. One contemporary saw in the waters of Hellbrunn "the essence of Venice".

THE PALACE

Visiting Hellbrunn by car, one goes from the car park straight into the *cour d'honneur* (main courtyard). It is a better idea, though, to take the time to approach the palace from the direction of the Hellbrunner Allee, by the old driveway, for only then can the Manneristic aim of "surprise" be realised. The avenue (Allee) follows its apparent direction *past* the Palace, and the visitor is for a time uncertain where he is heading for, until right at the end, when, after a sharp bend, there stands the Palace, suddenly and unexpectedly, before him. A long, narrow drive lined with outbuildings leads into the main courtyard; the gardens are not yet visible, being screened off by walls.

In the grotto under the flight of steps up to the main door, the leitmotiv of Hellbrunn is already introduced: Bacchus, in the shape of a water deity with two ibexes (the heraldic beast of the Archbishop). Hellbrunn is an aquatic "pleasure-ground", governed by Bacchus; here time flows by in Bacchic revels, just as water takes on multifarious forms as it flows. The ibex is a reminder of the builder; in the zodiac, it is one of the water signs (Capricorn), and belongs here, along with tree and water spirits, to Bacchus' entourage. It lends its name to the ancient dramatic form of tragedy (Gr. trágos = goat, ōidé = ode); we shall return later to the subject of theatre in Hellbrunn. But first to the grottoes: they are the approaches to Hades, the realm of the Dead — Orpheus the bard took this path when he made his attempt to bring his wife Eurydice back to life — and offered the baroque-age melancholic the opportunity for contemplation.

Before turning to the grottoes and fountains, one should visit the state rooms of the Palace. A steep staircase leads up to the great hall, the walls of which are covered all the way round with scenes by Donato Mascagni, who also did the frescoes in the Cathedral. Illusionistic painting gives the visitor the impression of wandering through a hall of pillars with views on to busy streets and squares. Gilded statues of Roman emperors stand at each end, and allegorical female figures enliven the galleries. In the centre of the ceiling, above the illusionary architecture, hovers a spirit. This room is dominated solely by architecture constructed by human hand, with open sky arching above it. The adjoining room,

Murals in the Octagon of Hellbrunn Palace

with its lofty dome, is the Octagon. The actual walls are once more removed, as it were, by trompe l'oeil architecture. This room is entirely decked in lavish blue and gold, with only small gaps admitting glimpses of the sky. In spite of the painted corridors, this architectural fantasy gives a hermetic and labyrinthine impression — a meeting-place for cavaliers and their ladies. Legend has it that the young man presenting a carnation to a girl is in fact the Archbishop himself. In the dining-room with the fine tiled stove (1608) by Friedrich Strobl (it was altered under Marcus Sitticus and moved here) hangs a portrait of the Archbishop, by Donato Mascagni (1618). Here, against the background of Hellbrunn Palace and Gardens, Marcus Sitticus is holding up a picture of the Cathedral, still under construction. The other painting shows Hohenems, the birthplace of Marcus Sitticus. The walls of the "Tapetenzimmer" are covered with 18th century Japanese wallpaper. In the vestibule hang paintings portraying wonders of nature — rare, misshapen or gigantic animals.

WASSERSPIELE (the fountains)

These can be visited only on a guided tour. The many sculptures were executed by Hans Waldburger, Esaias Gruber and Andreas and Hans Pernegger, all from Salzburg, and by the Italians Hieronymo Preosto and Bernardo Zannini. The main figures are attributed to the sculptor and architect Santino Solari.
Behind the palace are the still pools, the grottoes, a theatre, water-operated moving figures and fountains. The visitor is kept in a constant state of nervous expectancy, now scared, now amused, alternating between light and shade as he escapes from the dark caves into the sunlight. But even in the open, he has no peace of mind, for another shower may take him unawares, and he has to keep moving. There are plenty of places to suit a melancholy mood — springs and grottoes where Neptune rules or Orpheus sings, where ibexes emerge from the water; but the first symptoms of melancholy are promptly dispelled by diverting aquatic tricks. It was supposed to be dangerous to fall asleep near a spring or a well, which were gateways to the Underworld; there is no risk of this here, for the trick fountains, like the water-spirits, are capricious, mischievous and cunning. Not even the reveller, overcome at last by wine and drowsiness, will find peace here, for the jet of water issuing from the stool he is sitting on recalls him quickly to the present moment. The fountains prevent the senses from growing numb, and set them free on the wings of laughter.

THE PLEASURE-GARDEN

This is adjacent to the Wasserspiele, but can also be entered free from the Palace. The island in the carp-pond had a hill with a pavilion and a grotto until the modifications made by the inspector of the gardens, Franz Anton Danreiter, around

The "Wasserspiele" in Hellbrunn: the "Roman theatre" with its stone table

1730. On the Hellbrunner Berg stands the "Monatsschlössl" (Monat = month), also called Waldems, which Marcus Sitticus is said to have built in record time in 1615, having mustered all the masons of the archbishopric. Today it houses a folklore museum.

The outer park extends a lot further eastwards; until the end of the 18th century, there was a belvedere, and hermitages occupied by anchorites. Marcus Sitticus had a quarry in the hillside converted into the Steintheater (stone theatre), reputedly the oldest romantic natural theatre in the German-speaking world; the first performances, north of the Alps, of Italian operas were given here, during the reign of Marcus Sitticus. This art of the "dramma per musica", just flowering in Italy at the time, was especially cultivated at the court of Salzburg. Performances of "Orfeo" by Claudio Monteverdi, of an "Andromeda" and of "Pastorales" are reported. The figures from classical mythology in the grottoes, theatres and springs of the Wasserspiele were certainly inspired by these performances.

Behind the hill lies the zoological garden, the natural successor to the archiepiscopal game preserve. Here grazed white stags, which had to be consigned to Vienna after the secularisation of the archbishopric.

The Hellbrunner Allee (Hellbrunn Avenue): The Salzburg aristocracy erected their villas and palaces along this avenue; these are privately owned and not open for viewing. The avenue begins beside Schloss Freisaal (no. 12, Freisaalweg) in Nonntal. Here, in the great hall, is preserved a series of frescoes dating from 1558. Schloss Frohnburg (no. 53, Hellbrunner Allee) was built, starting in 1672, by the Kuenburg family; today it is a student hostel for the Mozarteum Academy of Music. The fountain of Arion at the entrance is worthy of note; the musician Arion had escaped by jumping into the sea from the sailors who intended to rob him, and a dolphin carried him safely to land. The Emsburg (no. 52, Hellbrunner Allee), built in 1618, was the seat of the Mabon family; the Order of Knights of St. Rupert was based here from 1701. Schloss Emslieb (no. 65, Hellbrunner Allee) was built by a nephew of Marcus Sitticus in 1618, but underwent alterations in the 18th century.

Maria Plain

Maria Plain is a place of pilgrimage dedicated to the Virgin Mary. The church was elevated in 1952 to the rank of Papal Basilica Minor. The miraculous image, a painting of the Virgin with Child, had in 1633 miraculously survived undamaged a fire in the Bavarian town of Regen, and was consequently venerated as being able to work miracles. A Salzburg family brought the picture to their estate in Plain, where it was put on display in the "Ursprungkapelle" (beside the present hotel). The influx of pilgrims finally led to the building of the church in 1671, under Archbishop Max Gandolf Kuenburg. Wolfgang Amadeus Mozart is said to have composed the "Coronation Mass" in 1779 for the 28th anniversary of the solemn crowning of the picture with a votive crown; more recent researches, however, relegate this information to the realm of legend.

The architect Giovanni Antonio Dario had taken as his model the cathedral façade, and created a building designed to be looked at from a distance. The sculptures of the Four Evangelists in the niches are attributed to him.

Decoration and furnishings: The decoration and furnishings of this barrel-vaulted church with partitioning interior buttresses is, owing to the many pious bequests, extremely rich. The magnificent high altar, which dates from the time of building, shelters the miraculous image in a silver frame and an aureole. The statues of SS. Vitalis and Maximilian are the work of Jakob Gerold, and the painting of the Holy Trinity in the upper part is by Frans de Neve. The right-hand altar (1673) of the triumphal arch has sculptures by Thomas Schwanthaler and paintings by Frans de Neve (the Wedding of the Virgin Mary). The sculptures on the left-hand altar (1674) were executed by Bartholomäus Opstal; the painting of the Crucifixion, by Roethiers, dates from 1744. The beautifully-worked screen with angels and grotesque work is a masterpiece by Hans Thoma (1683). The free-hanging sculpture of the "Queen of the Rosary" is by an unknown artist (1675). The Pietà, the Immaculata, the Christ in Agony, and SS. Gertrude and Nepomuk are works by Simon Fries, from around 1730.

The chapel altars: These were installed between 1675 and 1689, and have fine sculptures by Thomas Schwanthaler (3rd chapel, the St. Benedict or Holy Sacrament altar; 4th

chapel, the altar of the Holy Family), Simon Fries (1st chapel, altar of the Holy Family)
and Wolf Weissenkirchner (2nd chapel, altar of the Fourteen Votive Saints).
Martin Johann Schmidt painted the bell-shaped pictures beside the triumphal arch altars
and in the side chapels, in 1765 (with scenes from the lives of SS. Benedict, Wolfgang, Mau-
rus and Placidus). The pulpit, painted in grisaille, was donated in 1682.

Klesheim Palace

Archbishop Johann Ernst Thun entrusted Fischer von Erlach with the planning of this country seat. It was built in 1700—1709, but had to undergo alterations and was not ready for occupation until 1732, during the reign of Archbishop Leopold Anton Firmian. The centre section was planned with vestibule
and loggia, but Archbishop Thun demanded that the open arcades be closed and
given smaller windows. The covered ramp and terrace were added by Archbishop Firmian; the stags with star-studded antlers are his heraldic beasts. The
palace is used to accommodate official guests of the Province of Salzburg, and
is not open to visitors. In the park stands the charming "Hoyos-Schlössl", a
small summer-house with an interesting ground-plan, designed in 1694 by
Johann Bernhard Fischer von Erlach.

Anif Castle

This attractive moated castle was constructed in 1838—1848, under Count Alois
Arco-Steppberg, on the site of an older building, in accordance with the romantic ideals of castle-building. Castle and park are privately owned, and are not
open to visitors.

The Palace of Leopoldskron

Archbishop Leopold Anton Firmian had this palace built at the edge of the old
cow-pond in 1736—1744, as a family seat, and his nephew Franz Laktanz lived
in it with his family. The plans were drawn up by Father Bernhard Stuart, a
monk from the Scottish Benedictine monastery of St. Jakob, in Ratisbon, and
professor of mathematics at the University of Salzburg. The detailed sketches
are by the stuccoer Johann Kleber. The palace was built three storeys high, with
a mansard roof and a small octagonal tower in the centre. In the years preceding
1763, modifications in classical style were carried out; tower and mansard roof
had to make way for an attic storey in order to give the building a solid, rectiline-
ar appearance. The interior is richly decorated with stucco-work by Johann Kleber and his journeymen Benedict Zöpf and Johann Georg Braun. Franz Laktanz Firmian had assembled in Leopoldskron a famous art collection, which his
successors, however, sold in 1837, along with the palace, to the proprietor of a

The Palace of Leopoldskron with lake, and the Fortress

drinking-booth, who put an inglorious end to it. Pictures and furniture were sold off dirt cheap, books pulped down, the plaster casts of antique sculptures pulverised. In 1918, Max Reinhardt acquired the palace and made it into a social and cultural meeting-place in the early days of the Salzburg Festival. The palace is privately owned, and is not open to visitors.

Brief history of the building: Construction began in 1736, to plans by Father Bernhard Stuart; the detailed sketches and designs for decoration were supplied by the stuccoer Johann Kleber, and owed much to the forms of decoration used by Hildebrandt. Stuccoing by Kleber and his journeymen Zöpf and Braun was started in 1738. The building process was accompanied by lawsuits between Stuart and Kleber; in 1740, the Régence-style ornamentation of which Kleber was so fond was termed "old-fashioned". The chapel was consecrated in 1744. Modifications in classical style were carried out before 1763. The paintings in the great hall are by Andreas Rensi ("Four Seasons", c.1740) and Franz Anton Ebner (two Apotheoses of the Firmian Family, c.1736, and the ceiling painting of the Wedding of Atalanta, 1740).

SALZBURG   Oskar Anrather
RESIDENZ VERLAG

Deutsch [3-7017-0864-9]
S 590,- / DM 81,- / SFr 73,50
Englisch [3-7017-0890-8]
S 680,- / DM 98,- / SFr 92,-

Residenz Verlag